Caro's Most Loved & Admired House

The W. J. Moore House

By Mark Putnam

June 21, 2024

Dedications & Acknowledgements

This book is dedicated to today's Moore family, who have done so much to uphold and sustain the physical structure of the W. J. Moore House and the memories and artifacts of this storybook, this fairytale, house.

They likewise contributed a voluminous amount of pictures and narratives for this book.

I, too, dedicate this work to my grandfather, Claude Putnam, and his descendants. Claude, born in 1879, and his sons laid the stonework, the stone masonry, for the W. J. Moore House from 1923 to 1927—that included the stone walls, fireplaces, drive and walkways, and pillars.

During the same period, Seymour Kelly was a leader who transformed the old Dr. Olin House into the W. J. Moore House. Kelly aided the change that made the W. J. Moore House into a fairytale, or storybook, house that it is still today.

The W. J. Moore House is an intimate experience. It allows us to gaze and look at the early spirit, the early history, of the City of Caro . . . one hundred years ago.

Visiting the W. J. Moore House is like taking a fantastic, a large, step backward in time to the roaring 1920s, a time of vast economic prosperity and great, joyful, and superb exuberance.

Considerable portions of the treasured information found in this work came from the Caro Area District Library and the Digital Archives. Another invaluable online service is the Tuscola County Register of Deeds.

Perhaps, the greatest resource for information, a storehouse that is almost forgotten, is old newspaper issues published by the Tuscola County Advertiser that are now at the Caro Area District Library and are digitalized and put online.

Without these remarkable resources and their acts of preservation, protecting and defending information that is historical, the work in writing *Caro's Most Loved & Admired House—the W. J. Moore House*—would not be possible. These resources are greatly, highly, valuable.

Thank you all.

Contents

Epilog..6

123 North Almer Street—The Fairytale House......................................8
   The Legal Description...8

Michigan...10
   The Saginaw Treaty of 1819...10
   Sanilac County...10
   Land Survey...10
   Michigan Statehood..10

Tuscola County..12
   Organization of Tuscola County..12
   Self-governing of Tuscola County...12
   Indianfields Township...12

Samuel P. Sherman & Ruth W. Delling—S ½ of NW ¼, Section 3—Centreville..14

Melvin B. & Clarissa Gibbs—S ½ of E ½ of NW ¼, Section 3—Centreville.........16

Elizabeth Gamble—[S] 2/3 of Lots 2 & 7 and Lots 3 & 8, Block 9......................20

Plat of Centreville—Section 3—Now the City of Caro......................................22

Alexander P. & Jane Cooper—Lots 1 & 6, and N 1/3 of Lots 2 & 7, Block 9......24

Harvey Palmer—Lots 1 & 6 and N 1/3 of Lots 2 & 7, Block 9.............................26

Jefferson & Jenette Wilder—Lot 6 & N 1/3 of Lot 7, Block 9..............................26

Albert W. & Nettie Bradford—Lots 6 & N 1/3 of 7, Block 9................................27

Elizabeth Gamble—Lots [S] 2/3 of 2 & 7, and 3 & 8, Block 9..............................28

John W. & Jennie Boyd—Lots 3, 6, 7, & 8, Block 9...29
   Caro's Grist & Sawmill—South State Street...............................30

William & Mary Rose—Lots 3, 6, 7 & 8, Block 9..32

Lyndon & Alida Whipple—Lots 6 & 7, Block 9...33

Ebenezer & Olive Battelle—Lots 6 & 7, Block 9..34

Julian D. Wilsey—Lots 3, 6 & 8, Block 9..34

Alexander & Alice Reynick—Lot 7 & ½ of Lot 8, Block 9....................................35

Dr. James & Emma Graves—Lot 6, Block 9..36

William E. & Louisa Sherman— Lots 7 & N ½ of 8, Block 9...............................38

William H. & Emma Carson— Lots 3 & 7 and N ½ of 8, Block 9 40
Dr. Frederick & Nellie Bender—Lot 6, Block 9 42
Dr. Peter Livingstone— Lots 3 & 7 and N ½ of 8, Block 9 43
Dr. Richard & Nellie Olin 44
- The Olin Family in Caro 44
- The Olin House & Garage 46
- Olin Cars and Politics 48
- Nellie Jenks 50
- Sale of Olin House 50
- Lansing, Michigan 52
- Michigan State University 54

William James Moore & Lovila Ellen Wooley 56
- W. J. Moore's Early Life 56
- Initial Work 58
- W. J. Moore Companies 59
- Moore Interests 60
- De Dion-Bouton 66
- Cadillac Model 51 V8 - 1915 68
- Lovila Ellen Wooley 70
- Remodeling the W. J. Moore House 72
- Moore House Activities 78
- W. J. Moore House Remembered 80

Later Owners 86
- Andrew J. & Dolores Moore 86
- Charles & Dorcas Vaughan 88
- Linda & Kim Vaughan 89
- Melissa & Alvin Zavitz 89
- Steve & Becky Shields 90

Post Log 92

Epilog

Caro's Most Loved & Admired House—the W. J. Moore House—is one of the most iconic examples of Tudor Revival architecture, specifically within the Fairytale or Storybook style of architecture.

This whimsical style like Art Deco gained great popularity in the 1920s and 1930s, especially in places like Los Angeles, California. It was associated with the fantastic productions of silent and early talking movies.

Significant remodeling of the W. J. Moore House from 1923 to 1927 transformed a physician's house into a whimsical and extraordinary house.

Characteristic features of a storybook house are turrets or towers like those that are seen in another nearby stone house, the McDurmon or Hartman House, located just kitty-corner across North Almer Street from the W. J. Moore House.

Chuck Vaughan, a later owner of the W. J. Moore House, in the late 1900's, fulfilled a childhood dream. He purchased the W. J. Moore House . . . people than called it, affectionately, "Vaughan's Disneyland House."

The W. J Moore House is a special place in our hearts and minds. It conveys iconic symbols of beauty, freedom, and happiness. It conveys cherished memories that are very old and that will continue to last for generations.

The W. J. Moore House is the emblem of the City of Caro. It is a proclamation of what people hold in high regard. That is cheerfulness and happiness.

The W. J. Moore House is like an oasis in the desert, a retreat from an arid world.

One of Caro's largest water-wells that is still usable is located at the W. J. Moore House.

The W. J. Moore House is a wellspring, a retreat, that makes people feel carefree and happy.

It is a place of communication and rejuvenation.

It is a monolith. a monument, a stone pillar at an oasis at which we all gather around that indicates that life will be better.

Once upon a time, nestled in the heart of Caro, Michigan, stood a magnificent house known far and wide as the W. J. Moore House. Its history was woven with threads of magic and wonder, whispered through generations like a cherished secret.

The house, with its grand architecture and sprawling gardens, was said to have been built with dreams and aspirations by William J. Moore himself. Legend had it that every stone, every beam, and every tree planted on its grounds held a story waiting to be told.

In the glow of the morning sun, the W. J. Moore House shimmered like a jewel amidst the gentle rustling of leaves and the song of birds. Its windows gleamed with tales of laughter and joy, of families gathering by the hearth, and of evenings spent beneath the stars.

But as night fell, a different enchantment took hold. Moonlight danced on the walls of stone, casting ethereal shadows that seemed to whisper secrets of old. The ancient trees that stood sentinel around the house murmured ancient melodies, carrying memories of celebrations and solemn moments alike.

Visitors who ventured near the W. J. Moore House often spoke of a sense of peace that enveloped them, as if the very air held a tranquil magic. Some claimed they saw glimpses of figures from another time peering through the windows, their faces alight with joy and wisdom.

And so, the W. J. Moore House stood not only as a testament to craftsmanship and beauty but also as a living chronicle of a bygone era. Its fairytale spirit continued to weave its spell over all who crossed its threshold, ensuring that the magic of its story would endure for generations to come.

123 North Almer Street—The Fairytale House

The Legal Description

Arguably, the most magnificent, stunning, of houses, 123 North Almer Street stands out as Caro's most captivating and intriguing residence.

Over the years, it has been home to Caro's most exceptional and capable individuals, those who were guiding lights in an otherwise dark world.

Delving into the history of this remarkable place, you are struck by the impeccable taste of the various owners who called it home.

In its earliest days, before it was transformed into a fairytale house, it even then gathered attention. It was a prominent landmark that attracted the best of people and brought out the best in people.

Beginning in 1923, the era of booming economies, the house underwent a transformation. It acquired the aesthetic charm of a storybook, a fairytale, house.

The following description outlines the legal aspects of today's 123 North Almer Street address:

575-0051-000 SEC 03 T12N R9E LOTS 3, 6, 7 & 8 & N 1/2 OF LOT 9 BLK 9 ALSO, A STRIP OF LAND 37 FT WIDE OFF N END OF E 1/2 OF LOT 4 EX COM 33 FT S OF NE COR OF LOT 4, TH S 25 FT, TH W 21 FT, TH N 25 FT, TH E 21 FT TO POB ALSO W 1/2 OF ALLEY LYING E OF LOTS 1 & 2 BLK 9.
ORIGINAL PLAT VILL OF CARO.

Commonly called, "123 North Almer Street," the name "Almer" means essentially "High Born"!

It means the one who is grown up, the elderly, or alderman.

It means the "Elevation in the Marsh."

It means the place "High Above the Sea."

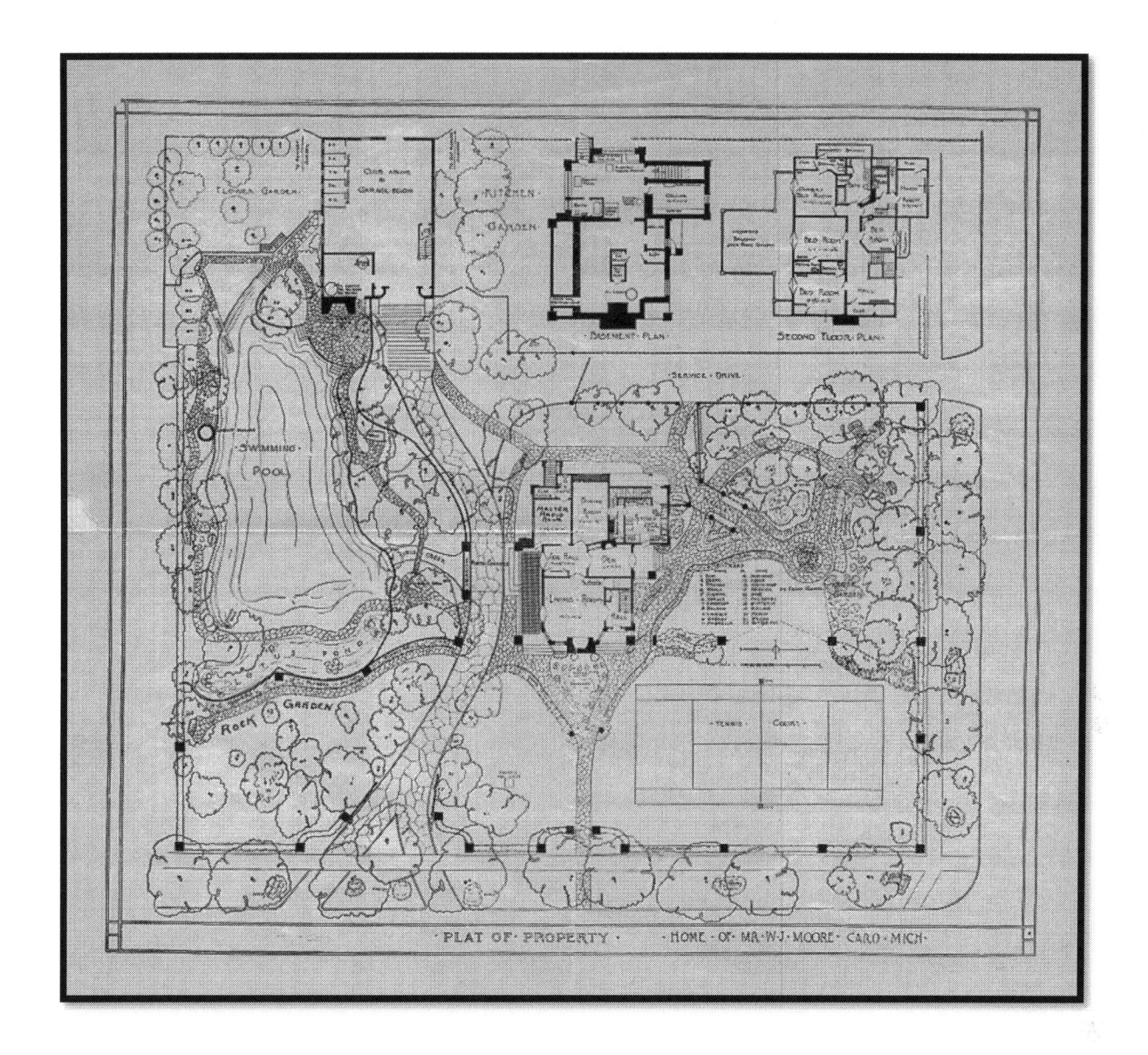

The plat for 123 North Almer, crafted by W. J. Moore, reveals more than just a property layout; it depicts a serene retreat nestled within a bustling world.

This thoughtfully designed space includes a shelter, providing a tranquil haven where one can escape the demands of daily life.

The shelter is not merely a physical structure but a sanctuary offering respite and rejuvenation. Whether it's a quiet corner for reflection or a gathering place for family and friends, the shelter at 123 North Almer embodies the essence of retreat, blending comfort and tranquility with the charm of early 20th-century design.

This plat highlights W. J. Moore's vision of creating spaces that cater to the soul, making it a cherished refuge amidst the chaos of modern life.

Michigan

Michigan was first inhabited by Indigenous peoples who made this land their home. They were hunters and gatherers who would often roam.

The Saginaw Treaty of 1819

In 1819, under General Lewis Cass and his soldiers, the United States acquired the northeast part of the lower peninsula in Michigan from the local Indigenous people through a cession or purchase agreement. The land encompassed Saginaw Valley, its tributary streams, and rivers, as well as the Cass River and included the area called the Flat Country, a part of which is now known as Tuscola County. The banks of the Cass River valley were filled with white pine timberland that made a picturesque and natural landscape.

Sanilac County

Originally, Tuscola County was part of Sanilac County. Sanilac County was established on September 10, 1822, by the Michigan Territorial Legislature. The boundaries of Sanilac County were adjusted in 1840, resulting in the creation of Huron County and Tuscola County.

Land Survey

In 1835, a survey took place of the area that soon would become Tuscola County. Following the completion of the survey, the United States initiated the sale of land in Tuscola County, starting from its western boundary and proceeding eastward. In the area, the survey marked the beginning of land acquisition and organized settlement.

Michigan Statehood

Michigan achieved statehood on January 26, 1837. It was the 26th state admitted to the Union. It held the distinction of being the only state in the nation comprised of two large peninsulas, the Upper Peninsula and the Lower Peninsula. These peninsulas were nearly surrounded by four Great Lakes. They likewise contain many other smaller bodies of water. [1]

---

[1] State of Michigan. About Michigan. Website.

General Lewis Cass and Indigenous leaders are pictured signing the Saginaw Treaty of 1819, a significant historical event that marked the cession of vast tracts of land in Michigan by the Indigenous peoples to the United States government.

This treaty, signed in the presence of various tribal chiefs, was a pivotal moment in the expansion of American settlements in the region.

General Cass, serving as the governor of the Michigan Territory, played a crucial role in negotiating the terms of the treaty.

The Indigenous leaders, representing their respective tribes, reluctantly agreed to the terms, which led to the transfer of their ancestral lands to the U.S. government.

The signing of the Saginaw Treaty was a somber moment, reflecting the complex and often contentious relationships between the Indigenous peoples and the American government during the era of westward expansion.

Tuscola County

Organization of Tuscola County

In 1840, the State of Michigan officially established Tuscola County. It was then an independent county. However, it remained judicially and administratively connected to Saginaw County for purposes that were governmental.

The establishment of Tuscola County as a separate entity marked a significant event in the area's history. The organization of Tuscola County occurred just three years after Michigan achieved statehood.

Self-governing of Tuscola County

In 1850, Tuscola County gained the ability to govern itself that signified a large step in its development. Tuscola County may have derived its name from Chief Otusson whose name may mean in the Anishinabek language "Level Land." The name Tuscola was created by combining Anishinabek and Latin roots, resulting in a word that was a hybrid. In Anishinabek, "desa" conveys "flat or level," while the Latin word "colo" signifies "cultivated land."

The heart of Tuscola County was the area called the Indian Fields, which played a crucial role in sustaining or feeding the local native population.

Tuscola encapsulated the concept of "Flat Cultivated Land."

Indianfields Township

The W. J. Moore House is situated in what was historically known as the Indian Fields.

It was renowned for its fertility and ability to produce food in abundance.

Native American people thrived in this area.

Being located on the Cass River and in proximity to the Saginaw Bay, Tuscola and Indianfields provided opportunities for productive fishing and hunting that enhanced the livelihood of the indigenous farming people in the area.

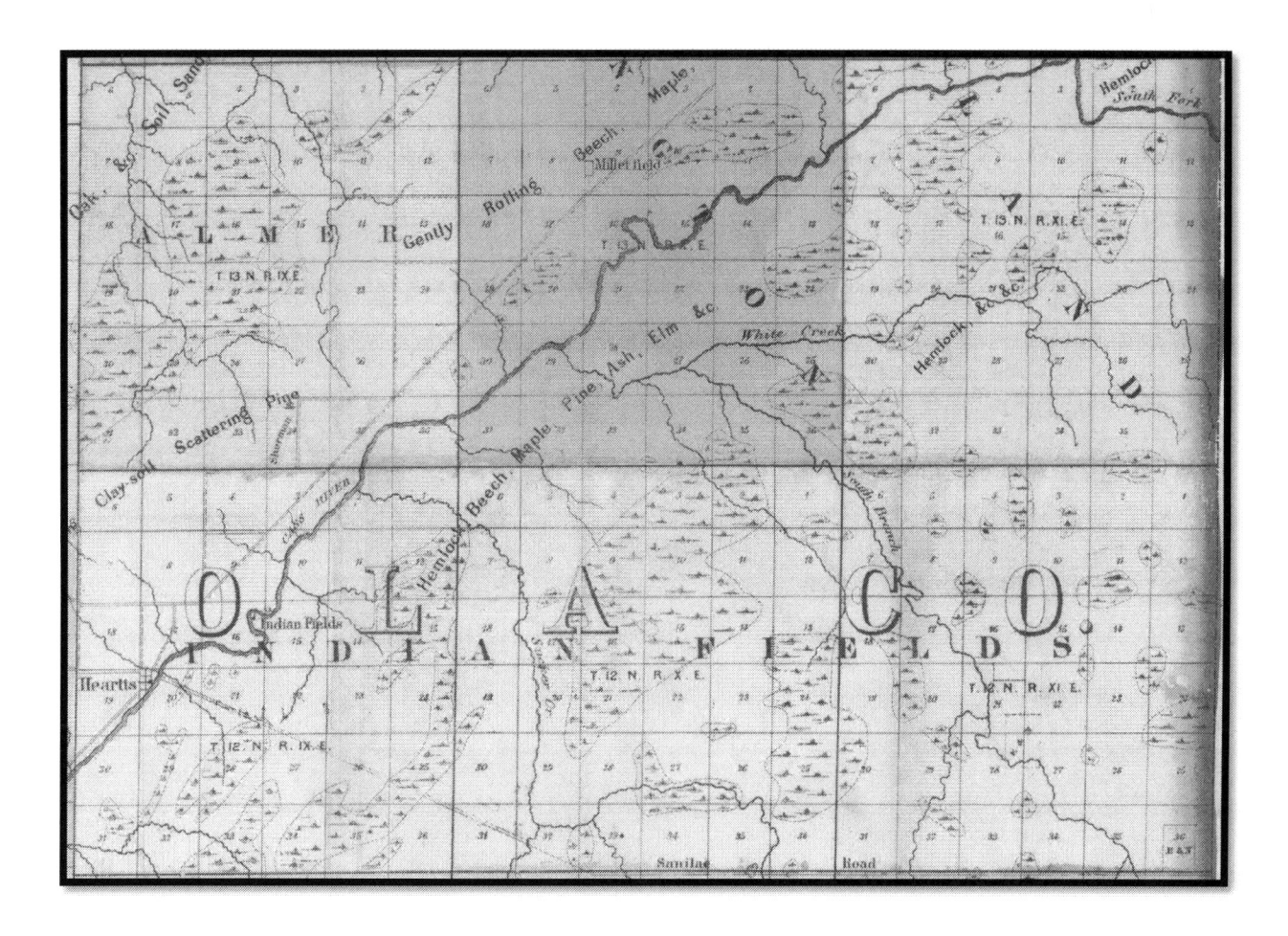

Almer and Indianfields, along with parts of Ellington and Elkland townships, are detailed on this map.

One notable feature on the map is the indigenous Chippewa Village, labeled as Indianfields in smaller type. This village was strategically located at a prominent geographic feature known as the "Sharp Bend in the Cass River" or the Oxbow, found in the lower left corner of the map.

The Oxbow, a significant natural landmark, served as a focal point for the Chippewa people, providing a rich environment for hunting, fishing, and gathering.

The map illustrates the deep-rooted connections between the Indigenous communities and the land.

The depiction of the village and its location on the map underscore the importance of the Cass River as a vital resource and a central element in the lives of the Chippewa people. [2]

---

[2] 1858 Tuscola & Saginaw Counties Map.

Samuel P. Sherman & Ruth W. Delling—S ½ of NW ¼, Section 3—Centreville

October 25, 1854, Samuel P. Sherman acquired an 80 acre parcel of land from the United States that included the site now occupied by 123 North Almer Street in Caro. The description of the tract indicated it was comprised of the South ½ of the Northwest ¼, Section 3. This land was a part of what later was called Indianfields Township. [3]

Tuscola County and Indianfields Township were characterized by varied topographies featuring both elevated hills, low points, and wet prairies.

Local Chippewa referred to this area around Caro as "High Bank" and "Ridge" that were known in their language as "Ishpadinaa." Early settlers may have anglicized it Ishpadinaa to "Podunk."

In the Eastern States, "Podunk" typically denoted a corner of land surrounded by marshy or low-lying land.

Within Sherman's white pine timberland that he would harvest for the logs lay the site where the William J. Moore House now stands.

May 17, 1858, Samuel & Ruth Sherman sold 20 acres of this land to Melvin Gibbs. This parcel was described as on the South ½ of the East ½ of the Northwest ¼, Section 3, T12N R9E [later Indianfields Township]. The transaction price was $300.[4] The land was feral, undeveloped, and lacked any dwellings.

Within seven years or in 1865, Melvin I Clarissa Gibbs divided their property into lots and blocks and as part of the in the Centreville Plat. Each lot was worth about $35.

The northwest quarter of Caro, or Section 3, was comprised of about 153 acres that Samuel Sherman purchased in two tracts.

The first tract was the North ½ of the Northwest ¼, Section 3. He purchased it from the United States in 1852. [5] The south tract, the South ½ of the northwest ¼, Section 3, Sherman purchased in 1854.

---

[3] Tuscola County Register of Deeds. Liber 1, Pg. 607.
[4] Tuscola County Register of Deeds. Liber 7. Pg. 162.
[5] 1875 Topographical Map of Tuscola. Snippet of Caro.

In 1852 and 1854, Samuel P. Sherman acquired two land patents for the Northeast ¼, Section 3, which is now part of the City of Caro. This strategic purchase laid the groundwork for future development in the area.

The "A" in "CARO" on the map above marks the specific location of the Gibbs tract, a significant portion of land that Melvin Gibbs purchased from Samuel & Ruth Sherman. This transaction is a key moment in the history of Caro, as it represents the early stages of land acquisition and development that would shape the growth of the City of Caro. [6]

---

[6] The 1875 Plat of Tuscola County. Beers.

Melvin B. & Clarissa Gibbs—S ½ of E ½ of NW ¼, Section 3—Centreville

May 17, 1858, Samuel Sherman sold a 20 acre tract of land to Melvin Gibbs. It was later a part of Centreville, now the City of Caro, and is now a highly prized residential section. The description was 20 Acres on the South ½ of the East ½ of the Northwest ¼, Section 3. The consideration was $300. [7]

At this time, the primary thoroughfare going north, and south was Almer Street. Soon, Frank Street was developed. Both Almer and Frank Streets served as half-section lines that determined the development of other streets in Centreville, now known as Caro.

In 1858, the State of Michigan constructed the Diagonal Road, the State Road, that now is M-81 and State Street in Caro. State Street intersected the crossing of Almer and Frank Streets to form a small town triangle.

In 1858, to house road workers, loggers, and incoming settlers, Melvin Gibbs erected Gibbs Hotel at the northwest corner of Almer and Frank Streets. The Gibbs Hotel, then called the Gibbs House, was substantial

The Gibbs Hotel served as Caro's first framed hotel. The Sherman Log Cabin previously was the place to stayover.

February 7, 1871, Melvin & Clarissa Gibbs sold to Elizabeth Gamble land consisting of the [South] 2/3 of Lots 2 & 7 and Lots 3 and 8, Block 9, and Lot 1, Block 13, The total consideration was $1,000. [8]

Elizabeth Gamble was the mother of Joseph Gamble. Joseph Gamble married Ruth Sherman who was the daughter of Samuel & Ruth Sherman. Joseph Gamble owned the local Gamble Grist & Sawmill.

At this time, vacant Lots in Centreville, now Caro, sold for about $35, so the cost of 4 2/3 lots was about $165.

There was a house valued at about $835 likely on Lot 7, Block 9.

---

[7] Tuscola County Register of Deeds. Liber 7. Pg. 162.
[8] Tuscola County Register of Deeds. Liber 25, Pg. 360.

This photo captures an early scene in the City of Caro, a glimpse into its burgeoning development during the late-19th century.

On the left stands the Gibbs' House or Hotel, a prominent structure built in 1857. This establishment served as a vital hub for travelers and locals alike, providing accommodations and a gathering place in a growing town. The Gibbs' House, with its welcoming facade, symbolized hospitality and was a cornerstone of Caro's early community life.

To the right of the image is the 10 Cent Barn, another significant structure in Caro's history. This barn, likely named for its affordable services or goods, reflects the practical and industrious spirit of the era. It catered to the needs of local farmers, tradespeople, and travelers, playing a crucial role in the town's economy and daily activities.

The intersection of Almer and Frank Streets, where these buildings stood, was a focal point of Caro's early urban layout. Almer Street would have been Caro's first main thoroughfare, bustling with activity as people went about their business. Frank Street, intersecting Almer, was added to the grid that facilitated movement and commerce within the town.

This scene, with its juxtaposition of essential community structures, offers a snapshot of life in Caro during its formative years. It reflects the architectural styles, economic activities, and social dynamics of the time.

Melvin Gibbs was a pioneer and settler of the early town of Centreville, which is now known as the City of Caro, Michigan.

As a significant figure in the town's development, Gibbs built the local Gibbs House, a hotel that offered rooms, food, and a bar.

The establishment provided essential services to travelers and locals, becoming a central hub in the community.

The Gibbs family's contributions to the town's early growth are commemorated with Gibbs Street, named in their honor, highlighting their lasting impact on Caro's history and development.

FOR SALE!

THE subscriber offers at private sale the following property:

Forty Acres!

Of Farming land within a mile of this village, mostly improved. A number of

VILLAGE LOTS!

and

Dwelling House and Barn,

In this village. Also

ONE MATCHED SPAN OF HORSES,

One Yearling Colt, 2 sets Harness, 1 double Wagon, 1 Two-horse Buggy, 22 Sheep, 9 Lambs, Plows, Cultivators, Fanning Mill, &c. Terms reasonable.

34m2*   MELVIN GIBBS.

The advertisement shown above was for Melvin Gibbs' property and was published on June 23, 1869.

The "Dwelling House & Barn" mentioned in the ad was likely located on what is today the W. J. Moore House property, indicating that a valuable and substantial home existed there from an early date.

Over the years, the property was also home to mill owners, physicians, and other prominent individuals, reflecting its historical significance and the importance of its residents in the development of Caro. [9]

---

[9] Tuscola County Advertiser. Jun. 23, 1869.

Elizabeth Gamble—[S] 2/3 of Lots 2 & 7 and Lots 3 & 8, Block 9

February 7, 1871, Melvin & Clarissa Gibbs sold property to Elizabeth Gamble that comprised [the South] 2/3 of Lots 2 & 7, and Lots 3 & 8 of Block 9, and Lot 1 of Block 13. The total consideration was $1,000. [10]

Lots 3, 7, & 8, Block 9, are the properties on which the Garage, the W. J. Moore House, and the swimming pool are located, respectively, today.

The 4 2/3 lots in this sale were worth about $35 each and in sum were $165. A house and barn were likely on Lots 7 & 3 and were built by Melvin Gibbs in 1869 or before. The value of these early buildings at these two locations, filled with promise and advantage, was about $835.

Elizabeth's maiden name was Huntley. She was born in Canda in 1815. She married David Gamble. Their son Joseph Gamble married Ruth Sherman, the daughter of Caro founders Samuel & Ruth Sherman. Joseph Gamble owned the Gamble Grist & Sawmill in Caro. The mill supplied crushed grain for food that fed settlers and lumber that was utilized in building homes and barns and businesses during the early development of Caro.

Joseph Delling and Joseph Gamble built Caro's first grist and sawmill about 1867. It was at West Creek and State Street. Delling sold the property and machinery to Gamble in 1869. [11] Lumber used in building the Gibbs House, later the Gamble House, likely, came from the early Gamble Grist & Sawmill.

On the 1870 Census, Elizabeth & David Gamble were one door away from Melvin & Clarissa Gibbs. The Gibbs Family then likely lived on the lot on which the W. J. Moore House now stands. The Gibbs House was built early in 1869 or before. The Gibbs House property likely included the "Dwelling & Barn" that Melvin Gibbs published for sale in June 1869 in the *Tuscola County Advertiser*.

Melvin & Clarissa Gibbs likewise sold 2 2/3 lots to Alexander P. Cooper. These properties were Lots 1 & 6, along Lincoln Street and [the North] 1/3 of Lots 2 and 7, Block 9.

The Coopers sold these properties to Harvey Palmer in 1866. Lot 6 today includes the grass tennis court that is just north of the W. J. Moore House.

---

[10] Tuscola County Register of Deeds. Liber 25, Pg. 360.
[11] Tuscola County Register of Deeds. Liber 21, Pg. 139.

The Gamble Grist & Sawmill, constructed around 1867 by Joseph Delling and sold to Joseph Gamble in 1869, was situated between Moore and Washington Streets at State Street.

While modest in its beginnings, it played a crucial role in the community's growth.

The site housed two mills: a grinding mill, or grist mill, and a lumber mill, or sawmill.

Initially, the sawmill operated with an upright saw that moved up and down rather than a circular saw.

Farmers brought grain from miles around to be processed at the grist mill.

The mills were powered by a waterwheel attached to a waterfall created by the elevated pond behind them.

In later years, the mills may have transitioned to using a steam engine for power.

Plat of Centreville—Section 3—Now the City of Caro

December 14, 1865, the founders of the City of Caro, then known as Centreville, officially platted the village.

The individuals who played a pivotal role in the incorporation of the municipality included Samuel P. Sherman, Ruth Sherman, Alexander P. Cooper, Stephen Cross, Peter D. Bush, Sarah Bush, Melvin Gibbs, Clarissa Gibbs, Charles Austin, and Fanny Austin.

Caro's development was greatly influenced by the presence of two creeks: Spring Creek, which was the east creek, and West Creek, whose original name is unknown. These two creeks formed the east and west borders of the early Village of Centreville, now Caro.

West Creek was the most viable and significant location for milling activity that produced flour and lumber. Flour fed settlers and lumber built Caro. Joseph Gamble along with Joseph Delling constructed Centreville's first grist & sawmill in 1867 at the intersection of West Creek and State Street.

The construction of a mill was foremost in the early stage of town-building, and a water-powered mill was the among the first structures built. Caro grew from the Gamble Grist and Sawmill. It was the vital center for milling grain and sawing lumber that would produce further economic activity.

Two creeks in early Caro were sources of power to early settlers, as energy could be harnessed from mill ponds and their falling water. Lumbermen likewise utilized creeks to transfer logs to the Cass River. The site of the Gamble Mill played a crucial role in the establishment and development of Caro and provided essential services and products that contributed to progress. Dams and bridges across State Street were at these two creeks. People first came to Caro by taking Almer Street and later State Street.

Reasonably, lumber for constructing the early homes on the site of the W. J. Moore House came from the Gamble Mill that utilized a dam, pond, and waterwheel for power from West Creek.

A similar operation likely took place at the intersection of Spring, or East, Creek and State Street where the past existence of the mill is seen in the name Millwood Street.

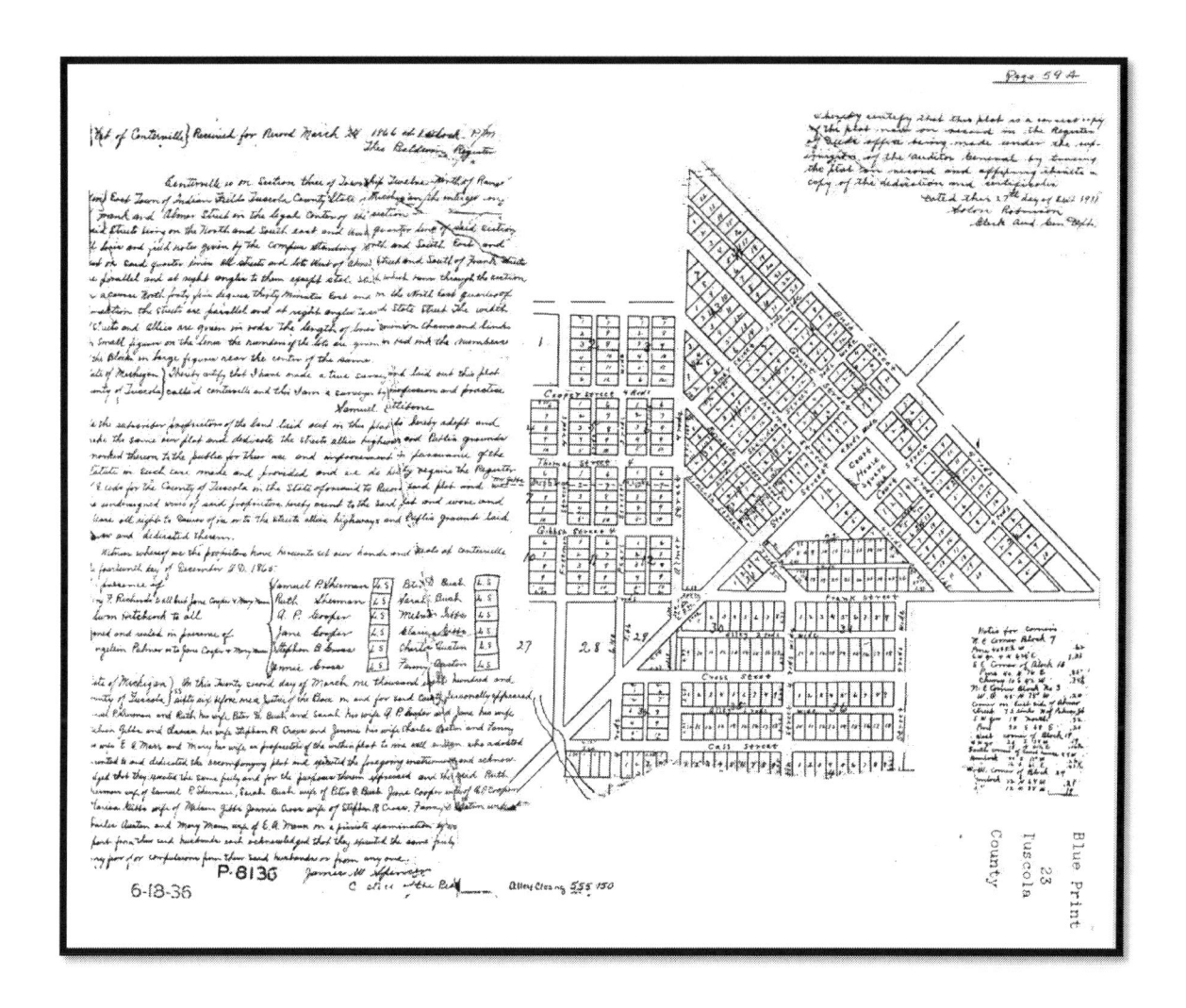

The original 1865 Plat of Centreville, which later became Caro, is depicted in the image above. It was delineated by two creeks, known today as West Creek and East Creek, which served as natural boundaries that were not easily crossed. Earliest access to the town was through North Almer Street.

The streets in the Centreville plat ran in different directions, determined by the specific quarter section they were situated in. Lumbermen selected their tracts based on these quarter sections, resulting in each quarter having different original owners. These quarter sections essentially dictated the layout of the streets.

In the northeast and southwest quarter sections, the streets mostly ran diagonally, while in the southeast and northwest sections, the streets ran laterally. When Centreville was platted in 1865, it is likely that dams were constructed where the creeks crossed State Street to serve as bridges.[12]

---

[12] Tuscola County Register of Deeds. Liber 1. Pg. 59A.

Alexander P. & Jane Cooper—Lots 1 & 6, and N 1/3 of Lots 2 & 7, Block 9

After the plat of Centerville, now the City of Caro, Alexander P. Cooper likely purchased Lots 1 and 6, as well as the North [1/3] parts of Lots 2 and 7, Block 9, from Melvin & Clarissa Gibbs. [13]

Alexander Cooper married Jane Sherman, the daughter of Samuel and Ruth Sherman who were the founders of the City of Caro.

Mr. Cooper was a partner in the firm of Washburn & Cooper that sold a variety of drugs and sundry items in early Centreville, now Caro.

Additionally, Mr. Cooper and his wife owned the Centreville Livery that was located adjacent to the Centreville House. They operated the stagecoach line that ran between Centerville and Vassar.

The Centreville House was Caro's first framed house that soon became a hotel or roadhouse. It is today the Caro Roadhouse Museum, a very noted landmark in Michigan's Thumb. In 1864, the Centreville House was "rebuilt." A new building was erected by Stephen R. Cross. It was on the same site that the old Centreville House stood and that today includes the Eclipse Hair Salon in Caro.

In 1864, the old Centreville House undoubtedly was moved and renamed. It then emerged as the Bush House.

May 7, 1866, Alexander and Jane Cooper sold Lots 1 and 6, along with the [North] 1/3 part of Lots 2 & 7, Block 9, to Harvey Palmer for $50. [14]

Harvey Palmer and his wife sold the property three years later.

Given the low payment amount that Palmer made, there was no building on this property at the time of the sale. The only building that was nearby was the Gamble House on the South 2/3 of Lot 7, Block 9.

When the plat of Centreville, now Caro, or December 1865, took place, all the lots in Caro were free of valuable, white pine, or Cork Pine timber. However, other less valuable trees, bushes, and stumps remained.

---

[13] Tuscola County Register of Deeds. Liber. Pg. Unknown.
[14] Tuscola County Register of Deeds. Liber 14. Pg. 56.

> **A. P. COOPER,**
> CENTREVILLE, - - - MICHIGAN.
> Proprietor of the Centreville Livery Stable, adjoining the Centreville Hotel. Single and Double teams, Heavy and Light carriages constantly to let.   1

The above advertisement for the Alexander P. Cooper Livery was placed in the *Tuscola County Advertiser* in 1868. [15]

During the 1860s and early 1870s, stagecoach lines grew to become the major and most popular means of public transportation.

In 1863, the Pine Run Stage scampered from Pine Run to Vassar. The Town of Pine Run was on the Saginaw Road, which followed the old Saginaw Indian Trail. The Saginaw Road went between Detroit and Flint. From Flint, it went on to Saginaw, Mi. In 1867, Joseph Garland, a resident of Pine Run, which was located a bit northwest of Flint, owned what was called the Tuscola and Vassar Stage Line.

In the middle of Tuscola County, a stage also came out of Centreville, now called the City of Caro. Centreville was so named because the village was at the center of Tuscola County.

This stage line was dubbed the Centerville & Vassar Stage Line, and its route was owned by Centreville resident Alexander P. Cooper who was the son-in-law of Samuel P. & Ruth Sherman—Caro's first permanent setters and founders. [16]

---

[15] Tuscola Advertiser. October 16, 1868.
[16] Thumb Wind. Internet. "Tuscola County Public Transportation – History Is Moving In The Thumb" Mark Putnam.

Harvey Palmer—Lots 1 & 6 and N 1/3 of Lots 2 & 7, Block 9

May 7, 1866, Harvey Palmer acquired Lots 1 and 6, as well as the North 1/3 of Lots 2 & 7, Block 9, from Alexander & Jane Cooper. The transaction was valued at $50 that indicates no house was on these lots. [17]

Subsequently, on March 18, 1869, Jefferson J. Wilder purchased Lot 6, along with the North ½ of Lot 7, Block 9, from Harvey Palmer. The consideration for this transaction was $150. [18]

No house likely was on these lots, but small improvements such as removing stumps or making the lots more accessible may have been implemented.

Jefferson & Jenette Wilder—Lot 6 & N 1/3 of Lot 7, Block 9

March 18, 1869, Harvey C. Palmer, hailing from Saginaw County, sold Lot 6 and the North 1/3 of Lot 7, Block 9, to Jefferson J. Wilder, a resident of Caro.

The transaction was settled for $150. About $100 was made plus Palmer, yet, owned Lot 1 & the North 1/3 of Lot 2, Block 9.

Jefferson J. Wilder was a lawyer by profession.

According to the United States Census of 1870, his personal property was valued at $1,500, while his real estate amounted to $2,000.

Jefferson Wilder served as the Clerk of the Tuscola County Board of Supervisors, now the Tuscola County Board of Commissioners.

It is likely that the Wilders built a house on what was later the north part of the W. J. Moore property, Lot 6, Block 9. There was a substantial increase in the property's value in the subsequent sale by the Wilders to their daughter and son-in-law the Bradfords.

---

[17] Tuscola County Register of Deeds. Liber 14. Pg. 56.
[18] Tuscola County Register of Deeds. Liber 20. Pg. 369.

The Wilders, then, constructed a house between 1869 and 1870 and soon relocated to Pasadena, California.

In 1871, the Wilders sold Lot 6 & the North 1/3 of 7, Block 9, to their daughter and son-in-law, Nettie and Albert Bradford for $1,500. The house had a market value of about $1,455, subtracting the $45 value of the lots. [19]

Albert W. & Nettie Bradford—Lots 6 & N 1/3 of 7, Block 9

October 9, 1871, Jefferson J. & Jennie Wilder transferred ownership of Lot 6 & the North ½ of 7, Block 9, in Caro, to Albert W. Bradford for $1,500.

Lot 6, Block 9, encompasses the tennis court area located today at the north end of the W. J. Moore House property.

The house built on this property about 1870 likely was one of Caro's most substantial buildings and was constructed utilizing lumber from the Gamble Grist & Sawmill.

The sale was a considerable increase in price for this property!

On July 8, 1874, Albert W. and Nettie Bradford sold Lot 6 and the North 1/3 of Lot 7, Block 9, to John M. C. Boyd for $420. [20]

The property at this time was worth about $375 with the price of the lots being $45.

John Boyd then owned the old Gamble Flour & Sawmill.

The Bradfords took a heavy loss on this sale of about $1,080.

There may have been a fire.

This property later would be owned by three different physicians. That suggests that it was a highly desirable and enjoyable location to its owners.

---

[19] Tuscola County Register of Deeds. Liber 28. Pg 165.
[20] Tuscola County Register of Deeds. Liber 36, Pg. 420.

Elizabeth Gamble—Lots [S] 2/3 of 2 & 7, and 3 & 8, Block 9

On February 7, 1871, Melvin & Clarissa Gibbs sold Lot 1, Block 13, and the South 2/3 of Lots 2 & 7 and Lots 3 & 8, Block 9, to Elizabeth Gamble. The consideration was $1,000. [21]

If the 4 2/3 lots were vacant, they would have been worth about $165. The average price for a Lot was about $35. By 1871, there likely was a "dwelling and barn" on the South 2/3 of Lot 7, & Lot 3, Block 9, that together were worth about $835. Lot 8 likewise was part of the plan and served as a pathway to the barn that had an outlet to the alleyway.

The Gamble House was one of Caro's first residential homes and possibly the first house built in Block 9. The house would have faced North Almer Street or the driveway that led to North Almer Street. This early home stood in the same location that the W. J. Moore House stands, today. The W. J. Moore House may have components of the original foundation and basement that possibly was dug and constructed about 1868 or 1869.

Elizabeth was the wife of David Gamble. About 1868, their son Joseph Gamble bought Caro's first grist & sawmill that was built about 1867 by Joseph Delling and Joseph Gamble. The mill was at the intersection of State Street and West Creek. West Creek was the west border of Centreville and ran from the top of the northwest quarter of Caro south to the Cass River.

The Gamble House on the South 2/3 of Lot 7, likely, was built by 1869 by Melvin Gibbs with lumber sawn at the Gamble Grist & Sawmill. It would have had a house and Barn made by Melvin Gibbs such as in his advertisement in the local newspaper that was published June 23, 1869. Centreville, later Caro, was platted in December 1865, before the house and barn were built.

These properties were the heart of Caro's earliest and best residential sections. They were part of the stage, the showcase, of domestic life in Caro. Here Caro's most influential and powerful people successfully would live and entertain. Here they would thrive and flourish.

April 2, 1875, Elizabeth Gamble sold "Caro's Best of Homes" to John M. Boyd or Lots 1, 2, 3, 8 & the of 2/3 of 7, Block 9. The consideration was $1,000. [22]

---

[21] Tuscola County Register of Deeds. Liber 25, Pg. 360.
[22] Tuscola County Register of Deeds. Liber 38, Pg. 129.

John W. & Jennie Boyd—Lots 3, 6, 7, & 8, Block 9

July 8, 1874, John W. Boyd, then one of the most opulent businesspersons in Caro, purchased Lot 6, Block 9, for $420 from Albert & Nettie Bradford along with the North 1/3 of Lot 7, Block 9. If the lots were worth $45 in total, the structure on this property was worth $375.

April 2, 1875, Elizabeth Gamble sold to John Boyd Lots 1, 2, 3, 8, the South 2/3 of 7, Block 9, for $1,000.

At $35 per Lot, the 4 2/3 lots, if vacant, were worth about $165 that leaves the "House and Barn" worth $835.

August 13, 1876, William Stewart of Macomb County, Michigan, for the estate of John & Jennie Boyd, sold William A. Rose of Tuscola County Lots 1, 2, 3, 4, 6, 7, & 8, Block 9, and Lots 1, 2, & 3, Block 34. The consideration was $1,800. [23]

The following is the breakdown of the $1,800 sale:

The ten lots, if vacant, had a value of about $350. That would leave improvements and buildings worth $1,450.

The old Gibbs or Gamble property, the "Dwelling and Barn," had a value of about $835 and was located on the South 2/3 of Lot 7, Block 9.

The old Wilder or Bradford House that degraded in value on Lot 6 & the North 1/3 of 7, Block 9, was valued at about $375. There likely were improvements on other lots in the 1876 transaction worth $240 or a profit was acquired.

The Boyd's bought the Allan Sheldon Flour and Sawmill that previously was the Gamble Mill. In 1876, the Boyd's sold the mill to Julian D. Wilsey.

Previously, in 1874, Albert & Nettie Bradford bought Lot 6 & the north 1/3 of 7, Block 9, from Nettie's parents, Jefferson & Jennette & Wilder. The Wilder's likely built a substantial house on this property between 1869 and 1871. In 1871, the Wilder's sold the property to their daughter and son-in-law for $1,500. When the Bradford's sold to John Boyd in 1874, they received $420, the Bradford's seemed to have taken a very heavy loss.

---

[23] Ibid. Liber 38, Pg. 623.

Caro's Grist & Sawmill—South State Street

The Gamble, Sheldon, Boyd, and Wilsey families played a pivotal role in the early development of Caro.

These families were instrumental in building homes and businesses that used lumber milled by their enterprises.

The earliest grist and sawmill in Caro were built by Joseph Delling and Joseph Gamble in 1867. In 1869 Joseph Gamble purchased the mill from Delling. It was then known as the Gamble Grist & Sawmill.

The mill later came into the possession of Allan Sheldon & Company from Detroit, Michigan.

Sheldon subsequently sold the mill to John M. Boyd & Company, which failed in 1876. The company then sold the mill to J. D. Wilsey & Company.

By 1883, the gristmill operated three grindstones, grinding about 50,000 bushels of grain annually.

The sawmill, though small, processed pine, hemlock, and various hardwoods into lumber.

The two mills employed approximately six people. In 1883, the sawmill's capacity was expanded with the addition of a circular saw.

Beyond producing lumber and flour, the mills' power also ran machinery for manufacturing furniture, such as chairs, and boxes.

In 1883, Julian D. Wilsey and Solon P. Spafford managed the business. They had initially been in business in Detroit but closed their operations there in 1878.

In 1876, they acquired the stock of John M. Boyd & Company, including dry goods, groceries, crockery, glassware, and hardware.

The purchase also included a brick block, thirty acres of land, and other Caro properties.

Wilsey & Company operated both the store and the mills. [24]

---

[24] History of Tuscola & Bay Counties, Michigan. H. R. Page & Co.,1883. Pg 91..

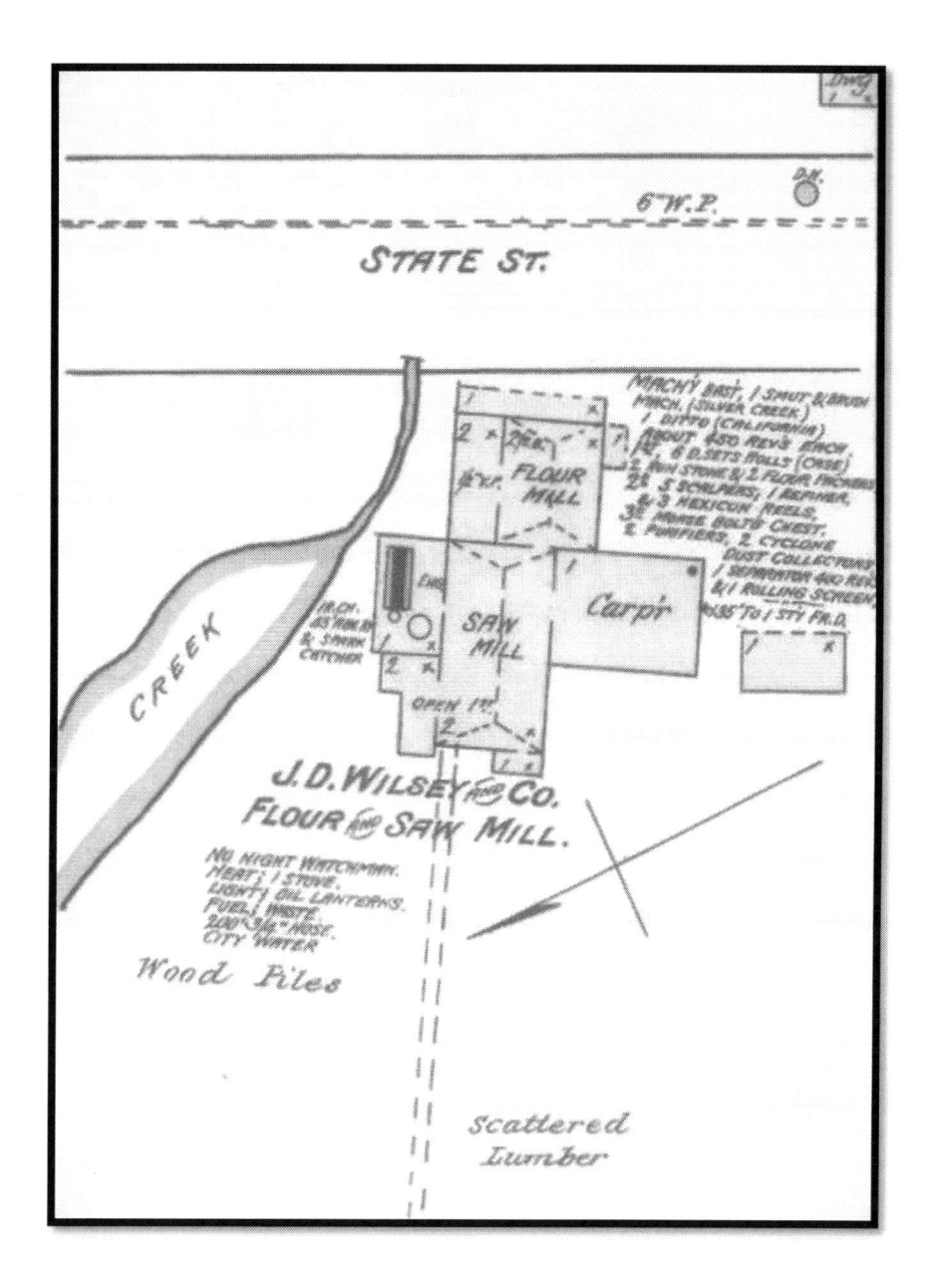

The Wilsey Flour & Sawmill in Caro was previously known as the Boyd Mill and, for a brief period, as the Sheldon Mill.

The earliest iteration was the Gamble Mill, originally built by Joseph Delling and Joseph Gamble. [25]

---

[25] The 1890 Sanborn Map of Caro, Michigan.

William & Mary Rose—Lots 3, 6, 7 & 8, Block 9

August 13, 1876, William & Mary Rose bought from the Boyd Estate Lots 1, 2, 3, 4, 6, 7, & 8, Block 9. Other lots in the purchase were Lots 1, 2, 3, Block 34. The price was $1,800. [26]

Mary Rose was the daughter of Ebenezer & Olive Battelle. [27]

At $35 apiece, ten lots, if they were vacant, were worth about $350. That leaves any buildings or improvements to be worth $1,450.

Lots 3, 7, & 8, Block 9, likely contained a "dwelling and barn" that were worth $835.

The house on Lot 6, Block 9, was worth about $420 less $45 for the lot or a total of 375. The $420 amount comes from the previous Bradford to Boyd sale. There remained improvements on the other lots totaling about $240 unless there was a gain or profit.

The South 2/3 of Lot 7, Block 9, was the foundation on which, later, Caro's most loved and admired house, the W. J. Moore House, would stand.

June 12, 1878, William & Mary Rose of Caro sold to Lyndon L. & Alida Whipple of Fairgrove—Lots 6 & 7, Block 9. The consideration was $1,300.

The two lots, if vacant, were worth about $70. The old Gibbs or Gamble House on Lot 7, Block 9, and the former Wilder or Bradford House on lot 6, Block 9, then had values totaling $1,230.

The first house was worth $835 minus the old barn at about $100, or $735 while the second house or improvement was worth $420 minus the lot at $45, or 375, making a profit or appreciation of $120.

William A. Rose married Mary Battelle. He died in 1879.

Mary Rose worked as a teacher. In 1885.

She died in Fairgrove a widower.

---

[26] Tuscola County Register of Deeds. Liber 38, Pg. 129.
[27] 1870 Gilford, Tuscola, MI Census.

Lyndon & Alida Whipple—Lots 6 & 7, Block 9

On June 12, 1878, William & Mary Rose of Caro sold to Lyndon Whipple of Fairgrove two lots—Lots 6 & 7, Block 9—on which stood two houses.

The purchase price was $1,300. [28]

The Rose's bought these Lots from the Boyd's.

Lyndon Whipple became postmaster and justice of the peace for Kinter in Tuscola County—he died in 1885.

August 9, 1878, Lyndon & Alida Whipple sold the two lots: Lots 6 & 7, Block 9.

The Whipple's sold these lots to the father of Mary Rose, who was Ebenezer Battelle. The price was $1,350 or a profit of $50 for Whipple's. [29]

March 25, 1880, Battelle sold 1 1/3 of these two lots: Lot 6 and the North 1/3 of Lot 7, Block 9:

He sold the property to his daughter Mary Rose for $1,275. [30]

The value of this property previously in 1876 was about $420 when John Boyd bought it from Bradford's. When the Boyd's sold it to the Rose's with other properties, the value remained about $420. The Rose's sold it to the Whipple's: the value throughout remained about $420.

The Battelle's certainly built a new or improved house between 1878 and 1880 on Lots 6 & the North 1/3 of 7, Block 9.

The previous value of this property was $420: subtract that from the current price or $1,275 leaves an improvement valued at about $855.

Lots 6 & the North 1/3 of 7, Block 9, was the place of exercise and the game of tennis later at the W. J. Moore House during its zenith. A fantastic place to visit and play and enjoy recreational spaces, The W. J. Moore House was a place like a resort with a tennis court and other conveniences.

---

[28] Tuscola County Register of Deeds Office. Liber 43, Pg. 441.
[29] Tuscola County Register of Deeds. Liber 32. Pg. 128.
[30] Tuscola County Register of Deeds. Liber 53. Pg. 215.

Ebenezer & Olive Battelle—Lots 6 & 7, Block 9

August 9, 1878, Alida & Lyndon Whipple sold their property Lots 6 & 7, Block 9, to Ebenezer & Olive Battelle for $1,350.

Ebenezer & Olive Battelle on March 25, 1880, sold Lot 6 and the North 1/3 of Lot 7, Block 9, to their daughter Mary Rose for $1,275. Mr. Battelle likely built a house worth about $1,225 on these lots that were worth about $50. The house was suitable to be owned later by three different physicians. [31] Mary Rose on September 1, 1880, while living in Gilford, Tuscola County, sold Lot 6, Block 9, to Dr. James Graves of Caro for $1,200. After he passed, Emma Graves, his wife, in 1904 sold Lot 6, Block 9, to Dr. Frederick Bender for $1,100.

Ebenezer Battelle may have sold the North 2/3 of Lot 7, Block 9, to Julian & Elizabeth Wilsey as on May 8, 1880, the Wilsey's sold to Alice & Alexander Reynick Lot 7 & the North ½ of Lot 8, Block 9. The consideration was $250. [32]

The Benders sold Lot 6, Block 9, to Dr. Richard Olin for $1,400 who would consolidate Lots 6 with 3, 7, & the North ½ of 8, Block 9. The Moore Family bought these properties when the Olin's moved to Lansing, Michigan, and after two intermediate transactions involving the Bliss Family and the Rachel McNair Estate took place.

Julian D. Wilsey—Lots 3, 6 & 8, Block 9

Emma & Charles Rose of Evart, Osceola County, Michigan and Mary R. Rose of Gilford, Tuscola County, Michigan, sold to Julian Wilsey Lots 1, 2, 3, 4, & 8, Block 9, and Lot 2, Block 43, for the consideration of $20 on August 25 and October 5, 1880. [33] [34]

Julian Wilsey sold Lot 6, Block 9 to James W. Graves, also, in 1880. The amount of $11.25 was the consideration. These may have been types of quit claim deeds as the dollar among was very low to what was agreed.

---

[31] Tuscola County Register of Deeds. Liber 53, Pg. 215.
[32] Tuscola County Register of Deeds. Liber 53. Pg. 410.
[33] Tuscola County Register of Deeds. Liber 52. Pg. 185.
[34] Tuscola County Register of Deeds. Liber 49. Pg. 143.

Alexander & Alice Reynick—Lot 7 & ½ of Lot 8, Block 9

On May 8, 1880, Julian Wilsey sold to Alice & Alexander Reynick Lot 7 & the North ½ of Lot 8, Block 9. This was the property that became the home of Dr. Olin and later W. J. Moore—the consideration was $250. [35] The W. J. Moore House property later was Lots 3, 6, 7, and the North ½ of Lot 8, Block 9. With the value of the lots at about $50, the value of the structure on Lot 7 and the North ½ of 8, Block 9, was only $200. The Reynicks likely built a new house.

Alexander Reynick was born in Ireland on February 11, 1832, and with his parents came to America. They moved to Wyoming, New York, after they first lived in Canada. Alexander Reynick married Alice Whiteside, and in April 1870, they came to Caro. When they arrived in Caro, it was no more than a hamlet, and Mr. Reynick first worked as a shoemaker. Eventually, he became the local justice of the peace, was a Trustee for many years in Caro, and was a local law and policy maker and enforcer.

Initially, like many others, the family attended Methodist Church services at Nettleton's Hall. The Reynick family was instrumental in building the first Methodist Church. They worked in the construction and maintenance of what to them was the "New Building." Alexander Reynick always gave a testimony that was stirring.

About 1880, with his failing health, he gave up his shoe business and directed his efforts to another call. Mr. Reynick turned to the pension and justice business that for 25 years he admirably conducted. Likewise, he served as chaplain of the Whiteside Post of the Grand Army of the Republic.

The Reynick family owned the building next to the Ellis block that once housed the "Karo Knovelty Kandy Kitchen." The Michigan Trading Stamp Company also opened its store in the Reynick building. Later A. C. Wilson moved his barber shop from Hotel Montague to his old stand, the Reynick building. The Reynicks during their later years lived on West Lincoln Street. [36]

On November 16, 1891, Alice Reynick sold to William Sherman Lots 7 & ½ of 8 for the consideration of $2,500. [37] Ten times what the Reynicks originally paid for the property; they likely had built a new house.

---

[35] Tuscola Register of Deeds. Liber 53. Pg. 410.
[36] Tuscola County Advertiser. Obituary.
[37] Tuscola County Register of Deeds. Liber 95. Pg. 160.

Dr. James & Emma Graves—Lot 6, Block 9

September 1, 1880, Mary Rose, a widower living in Gilford, Tuscola County, sold to Dr. James W. Graves of Caro Lot 6, Block 9.

The consideration of $1,200. [38]

For twenty-five years, the Dr. Graves family owned the north part of the property on which now stands the "Storybook House" or 123 North Almer Street. Dr. Graves was a prominent and well-known physician in Caro's early history. He was highly influential in the medical field and community service. Born in Ontario in 1845, he served as a physician in Caro for 38 years.

Dr. Graves arrived in Caro shortly before 1870. He established a practice and ran a small drug store.

Dr. Graves was kind-hearted, devoted, generous, and much more. Like many Caro physicians, his accounting books showed numerous unpaid bills, as he often treated clients who couldn't afford to pay. His congenial nature earned him many friends. His face was a familiar sight to the early settlers.

The good doctor warmly welcomed people into his home and frequently visited clients in their rural homes. At the time, roads were typically made of corduroy wood or planks, making travel jerky and bumpy. Dr. Graves endured long, uncomfortable rides on horseback or buggy to care for the sick and needy.

Often, his only reward was the heartfelt gratitude and indebtedness expressed by those he helped.

Dr. Graves was a highly learned, experienced, and skilled physician. He passed away in 1901. At his funeral, the cultured mourned the loss of the "good gentleman," while the poor grieved for the "good doctor" who had shown them both philanthropy and empathy. He remains one of the most beloved physicians in Caro's history. [39]

December 6, 1904, after the passing of Dr. Graves, Emma Graves sold Lot 6, Block 9, to Dr. Frederick & Nellie Bender for $1,100. [40]

---

[38] Tuscola County Register of Deeds. Liber 54, Pg. 84.
[39] Tuscola County Advertiser. Obituary. Pg. 1.
[40] Tuscola County Register of Deeds. Liber 138. Pg. 173.

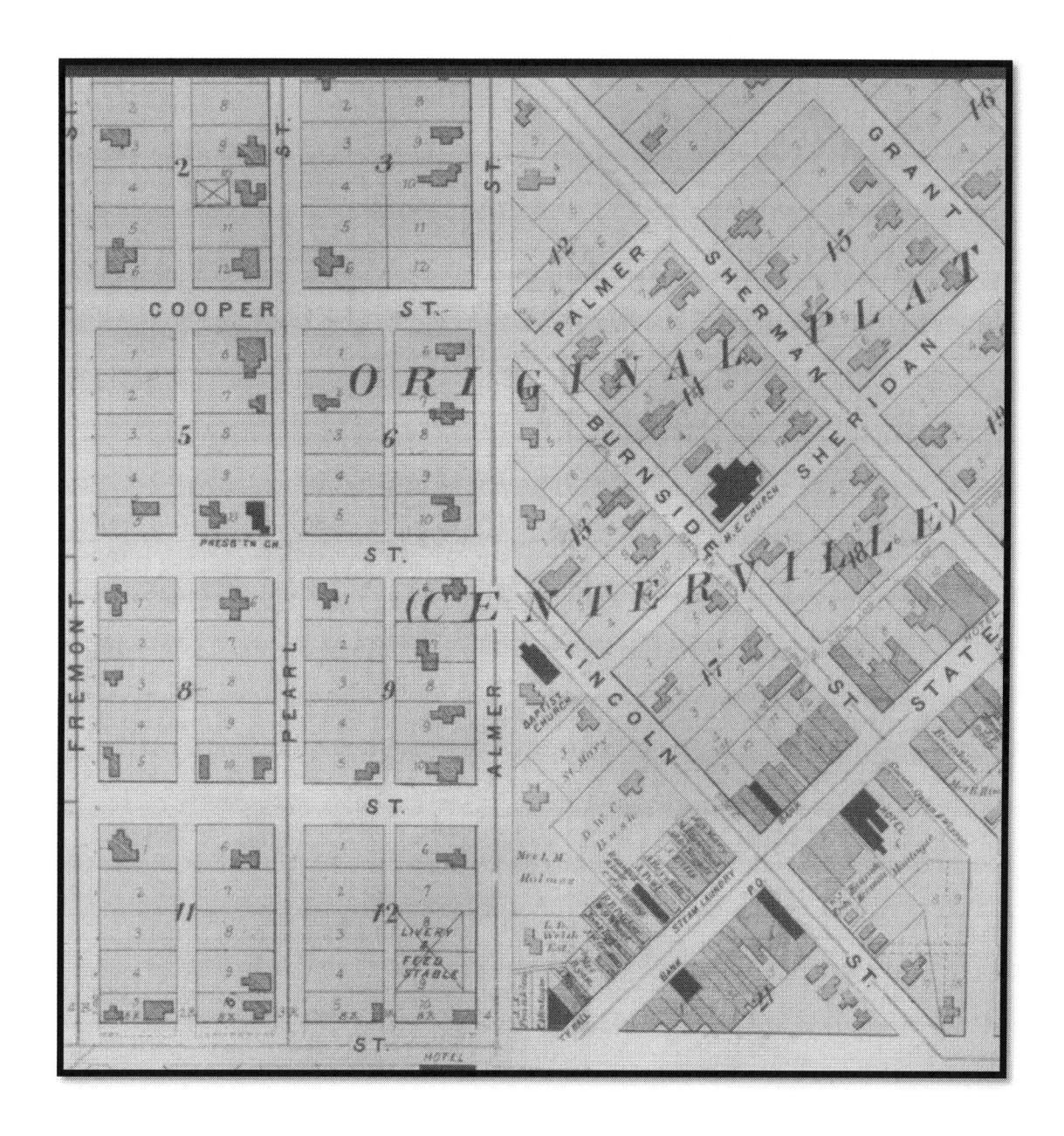

Near the "C" in Centerville was lot 6, Block 9, on which was Dr. Graves House.

This property and Lots 3, 7 & 8, Block 9, were the properties that included the Dr. Olin House.

It later was the storybook, or fairytale, home of the W. J. Moore family. [41]

---

[41] 1902 Plat Map of Caro.

William E. & Louisa Sherman— Lots 7 & N ½ of 8, Block 9

November 16, 1891, Alice Reynick sold to William E. Sherman Lots 7 & the North ½ of 8 for the consideration of $2,500. [42]

Between about 1857 to 1859, William Sherman, likely with his family, built Caro's first house, the Centreville House. This building soon served as a hotel, store, barroom, and temporary post office.

Today, the Centreville House is the Caro Roadhouse Museum.

Between approximately 1864 and 1870, Caro's first house was known as the Bush House or Hotel and was likely managed by DeWitt C. Bush, who was William Sherman's nephew through DeWitt's mother, Phoebe Sherman.

Around 1868, Clarissa and Melvin Gibbs, likely, built a house and barn on Lot 7, Block 9. An advertisement in the Tuscola County Advertiser on June 23, 1869, listed buildings as these two for sale.

On February 7, 1871, the Gibb's sold Elizabeth Gamble Lots 1, 2, 3, 8, and the southern two-thirds of Lot 7, Block 9.

Subsequent owners of the southern two-thirds of Lot 7 included the Boyd, Rose, Whipple, Battelle, and Reynick families, whom the latter eventually sold to William Sherman.

It appears that the Reynick House was rebuilt from what was originally the 1868 Gibbs House.

The Sherman House later became known as the Carson House and the Olin House.

In the 1920s, the W. J. Moore family transformed the dwelling into a storybook, or fairytale, house.

William Sherman, a member of the founding family of Caro, sold on March 15, 1895, Lots 7 & the North ½ of 8, Block 9, to William H. Carson who was part of the firm of Carson & Ealy. The price was $1,800. [43]

---

[42] Tuscola County Register of Deeds. Liber 95. Pg. 160.
[43] Tuscola County Register of Deeds. Liber 106. Pg. 434.

William Eber Sherman, who built the Centerville House, once owned the house and property where the W. J. Moore House now stands.

He was a prominent figure in Caro.

Along with his parents, Samuel and Ruth Sherman, he was one of the founders of the city. [44]

---

[44] Tuscola County Advertiser.

William H. & Emma Carson— Lots 3 & 7 and N ½ of 8, Block 9

William E. & Louisa Sherman of Caro, sold on March 15, 1895, Lots 7 & the North ½ of 8, Block 9, to William H. Carson who was a partner in the firm of Carson & Ealy. The consideration was $1,800. [45]

In the 1900 Indianfields [or Caro] Census, the William Carson family was listed next to his father-in-law, Nathan M. Richardson, and his then banking partner, John M. Ealy. By the 1910 Census, John Ealy lived at 343 North Almer Street. His home was next to Frederick McDurmon's residence at 302 that was across from what is now the Caro Presbyterian Church. The W. J. Moore House was located just south of the church. Although the 1900 census indicates that the Carsons were renters, this places the Carson family at 219 (now 123) North Almer Street, which later became the W. J. Moore House.

William H. Carson was born in Canandaigua, New York, in 1860 and moved to Caro in 1890 from St. Paul, Minnesota, where he had worked as a bookkeeper for a large firm. He purchased an interest in the abstract and banking firm of A. T. Slaght. Following the sale of Mr. Slaght's interest, the firm became Carson & Ealy. Carson dedicated himself to the business, and through his conservative business judgment, he gained confidence and friendships. Carson & Ealy rose from being third in banking in Caro to becoming the leading figure in the local banking scene.

With increased capital, the firm established branch banks in Fairgrove, Reese, Millington, Akron, Clifford, West Branch, and East Tawas. Carson managed the firm's real estate business, earning recognition as the local authority on real estate values.

In 1892, Carson married Emma Gertrude Richardson. In 1902, the Carsons completed their beautiful home on Wilmot Avenue [now West Burnside Street] at a cost of $12,000. The Carson & Ealy Bank eventually became the State Savings Bank. William H. Carson died on March 11, 1904. [46]

July 7, 1906, John M. Ealy, the surviving partner of the firm of Carson & Ealy, and his wife Bethany sold to Dr. Peter J. Livingstone Lots 3 & 7 and the North ½ of lot 8, Block 9. The price was $1 and other considerations. [47]

---

[45] Tuscola County Register of Deeds. Liber 106. Pg. 434.
[46] Tuscola County Advertiser. Mar 18, 1904. Pg. 1.
[47] Tuscola County Register of Deeds. Liber 145. Pg. 189.

The Carson & Ealy Bank was at the northwest corner of North State and West Sherman Streets in Caro—formerly the Slaght Abstract & Banking firm. [48]

---

[48] Tuscola County Advertiser. Ad date unknown.

Dr. Frederick & Nellie Bender—Lot 6, Block 9

December 1904, Emma Graves sold Lot 6, Block 9, to Dr. Frederick Bender. The consideration was $1,100. [49]

Dr. Frederick P. Bender graduated from the University of Michigan Medical School.

He married Nellie Adams, daughter of Dr. Albert Adams & Nancy Cessna.

Dr. Adams was a prominent physician in Belleville, Michigan.

The marriage of Dr. Frederick & Nellie Bender took place on September 14, 1899, in Bellevue.

They divorced twenty years later, on September 9, 1919.

In 1902, they moved to the Caro community, where Dr. Bender opened an office at 212 N. State St. in the Herman Block.

By 1913, he relocated his office to the new McNair Building, just across East Lincoln Street from the Herman Block.

Dr. Bender married twice more, before remarrying Nellie on July 9, 1925, in Ann Arbor, Michigan.

They divorced again on September 23, 1930.

Dr. Bender married for the fifth and final time in 1931.

On April 23, 1906, Dr. Frederick & Nellie Bender sold Lot 6, Block 9, to Dr. Richard & Nellie Olin.

The amount of $1,400 was the consideration. [50]

---

[49] Tuscola County Register of Deeds. Liber 138. Pg. 173.
[50] Tuscola County Registre of Deeds. Liber 141. Pg. 70.

Dr. Peter Livingstone— Lots 3 & 7 and N ½ of 8, Block 9

July 7, 1906, John M. Ealy, the surviving partner of the firm of Carson & Ealy, and his wife Bethany sold to Dr. Peter J. Livingstone Lots 3 & 7 and the North ½ of lot 8, Block 9.

The price was $1 and other valuable considerations. [51]

William Carson had acquired Lot 3, Block 9, separately from Lots 7 & the North ½ of 8, Block 9.

In one month for $5,500, Dr. Livingstone sold Lots 3, 7, and ½ of 8, Block 9, to Dr. Richard Olin, his partner in medicine.

Born in Ontario in 1864, Dr. Livingston's family settled in Cass City in 1881. After graduating from the University of Michigan Medical School, he moved to Caro, where he established a medical practice and became a significant figure in the local community.

Dr. Livingston served as chairman of the Tuscola County Medical Association, representing physicians in the area, and was well-known throughout Tuscola County.

In 1906, Dr. Livingston furthered his studies abroad. Upon returning, he worked as an ear, nose, and throat specialist in Detroit.

He passed away in Detroit in 1916, leaving a legacy In Caro and Detroit that was widely admired. [52]

It is likely that the old Reynick House was the framework for the new W. J. Moore House before it was transformed into a storybook house while later the Olin Family likely built the grand carriage house between about 1907 to 1909 that became the W. J. Moore House Garage.

On August 12, 1906, Dr. Peter J. Livingstone, a single man, sold to Dr. Richard M. & Nellie Olin Lot 3 & 7 and the North ½ of Lot 8, Block 9. The consideration was $5,500.

---

[51] Tuscola Register of Deeds. Liber 145. Pg. 189.
[52] History of Detroit. Dr. Peter Livingstone. Pg. 1093.

Dr. Richard & Nellie Olin

On April 23, 1906, Dr. Fredrick & Nellie Bender sold to Dr. Richard & Nellie Olin Lot 6, Block 9.

The consideration was $1,400. [53]

On August 12, 1906, Dr. Peter J. Livingstone, a single man, sold to Dr. Nellie & Richard M. Olin Lot 3 & 7 and the North ½ of Lot 8, Block 9.

The consideration was $5,500. [54]

The Olin Family in Caro

In 1905, the Olin family arrived in Caro. Dr. Olin, born in Perry, New York, in 1874, had recently come from St. Louis, Missouri, where he served as the superintendent of the Sanitary Commission for the World's Fair the previous year. There, he laid the foundation for the entire sanitation system.

He married Nellie Jenks.

Before moving to Caro, Dr. Olin practiced medicine for six years and lived in Battle Creek, Michigan.

Upon arriving in Caro, Dr. Olin rented the entire floor above what became the Olin Drug Store for his office and resided in Mrs. Hunt's House, located across from the Presbyterian Church. Despite sharing the same last name as Caro's druggist, Warren R. Olin, the two were not closely related and had never met before arriving in Caro. [55]

Dr. Olin quickly became an integral part of the community, eventually making his home at what is now 123 North Almer Street and what would become the W. J. Moore House. [56]

Dr. Olin was readily available for consultations at both his office and home. [57]

---

[53] Tuscola County Register of Deeds. Liber 141. Pg. 70.
[54] Tuscola County Register of Deeds. Liber 145. Pg. 189.
[55] Tuscola County Advertiser. January 20, 1905.
[56] Tuscola County Advertiser. January 27, 1905.
[57] Tuscola County Advertiser. March 24, 1905.

Soon after his arrival, Dr. Meredith sold his medical practice to Dr. Olin. [58]

Subsequently, Dr. Olin joined Dr. Livingstone's practice. Dr. Livingstone had been a well-established physician in Caro for many years and was a respected member of the community.

In his first eight months in Caro, Dr. Olin made a strong impression and quickly formed many friendships.

His deep understanding of "materia medica," demonstrated without any need for boastfulness, endeared him to the community, and earned him widespread respect.

The practice of Livingstone & Olin quickly became one of the county's most prominent medical businesses.

They consolidated their operations into Dr. Livingstone's office above Luce's Drug Store. [59]

In August 1905, a significant announcement in the local newspaper caused quite a stir throughout Caro and the surrounding county.

The drug store owned by W. O. Luce was purchased by druggists W. H. Olin & Son.

Previously, W. H. Olin & Son had been operating in the Mertz building in what was then called the Union Block.

Upon acquisition, they moved their stock and combined it with the W. H. Luce stock at their new location at the corner of North State and West Lincoln Street.

This consolidation reduced the number of drug stores in Caro from four to three, a number considered appropriate for a town of 2,500 people.

George H. Moore, Mr. Luce's clerk, was retained by W. H. Olin & Son and proved to be a reliable and valuable employee for the store. [60]

The apothecary shop later became known as the Moore Drug Store.

---

[58] Tuscola County Advertiser. May 5, 1905.
[59] Tuscola County Advertiser. August 18, 1905.
[60] Tuscola County Advertiser. 1905 or 1906.

The Olin House & Garage

April 23, 1906, Dr. Frederick & Nellie Bender sold Lot 6, Block 9, to Richard & Nellie Olin for $1,400.

On the property, over two years, the Bender's made $200.

In May 1906, people took note of the improvements Dr. Olin was making to the property previously owned by the late Dr. Graves and more recently by Dr. Bender.

The changes were so significant that the spot was scarcely recognizable.

Once the area was covered with grass, it became one of the most attractive corners in town, located on Lot 6, Block 9. [61]

During Christmas in December 1906, at the Presbyterian Church in Caro, Nellie Olin, Mrs. Holloway, and the Misses Pulver, Lange, Cool, and Wood performed delightful songs.

Doris Holloway and Ruth Ransford sang a beautiful duet, while Ms. Lane, Herman, Converse, Dickensheets, Smith, Van Sickle, Ostroh, and Case performed inspiring quartets.

Their performances were so well received that the large audience requested several encores, making the Christmas season very enjoyable. [62]

It is likely that the old Reynick House served as the framework for the later W. J. Moore House before it was transformed into a storybook house while the Olin Family built the grand carriage house between about 1907 to 1909 that became the W. J. Moore House Garage.

---

[61] Tuscola County Advertiser. June 25, 1906.
[62] Tuscola County Advertiser. December 6, 1906.

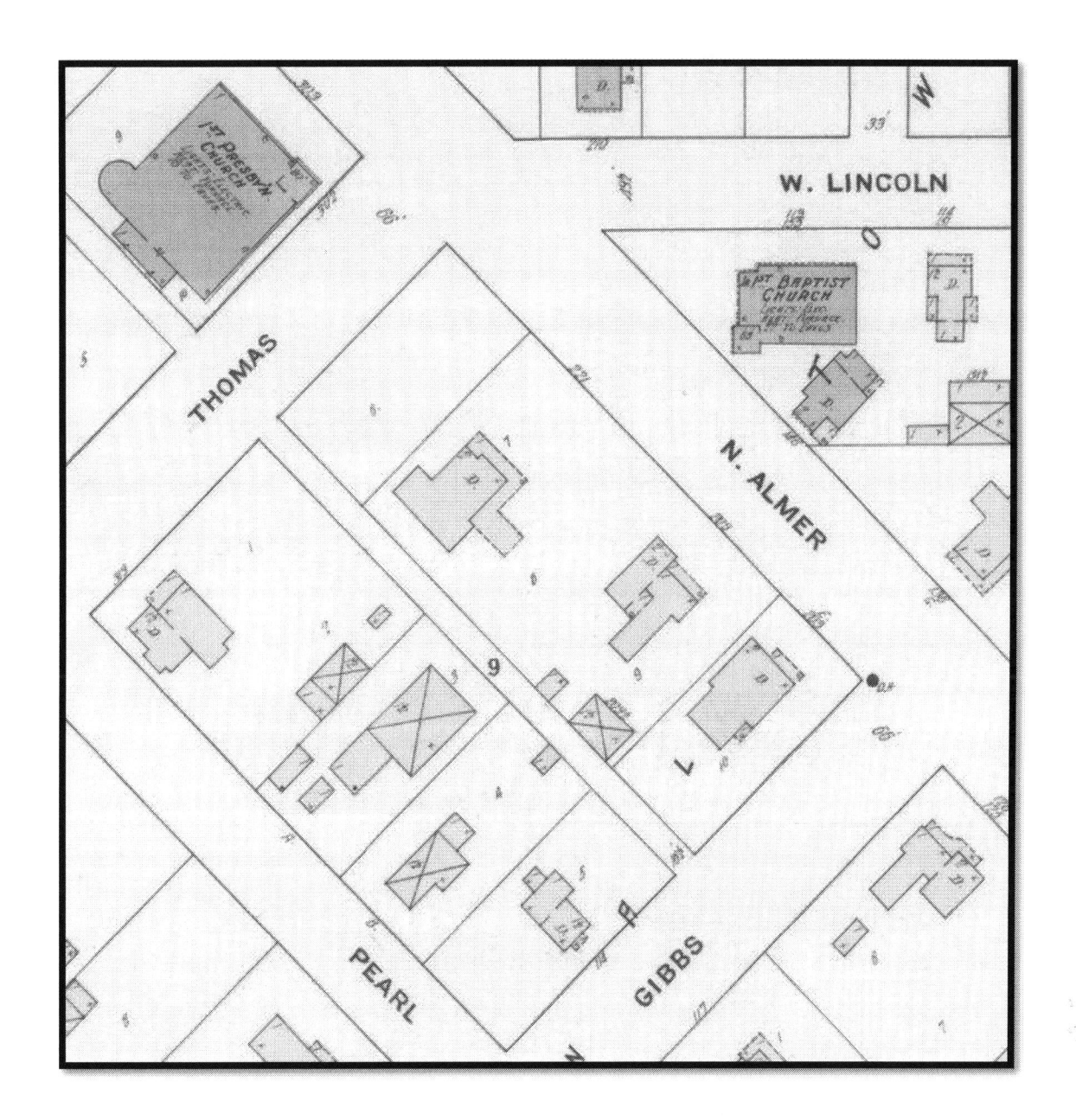

Dr. Olin's House and Property—Lots 3, 6, 7, & the North ½ of 8, Block 9, are seen on this plat in 1909. [63]

In 1902, there was a house on Lot 6, Block 9, and a house on Lot 7, Block 9, however, there was no carriage house on Lot 3, Block 9, in 1902. [64]

It is likely that the Olin family built the carriage house, now a garage between 1906 and 1909.

---

[63] 1909 Sanborn Insurance Map.
[64] 1902 Tuscola County Plat Map.

Olin Cars and Politics

June 1907, Dr. Olin purchased Dr. Handy's automobile. [65]

In July, he was seen driving one of the finest cars in Caro, a Thomas four-cylinder complete with all accessories and a top.

July 10, 1907, Dr. Olin was elected vice-president of the Tuscola County Medical Society, demonstrating his effective political engagement.

Dr. Olin's momentum continued. In March 1908, he was re-elected as a trustee for Caro and served on the town council until 1909. [66]

By 1908, Dr. Olin had retired from general practice to specialize as an eye, ear, nose, and throat doctor. [67]

He was soon elected as president of the Tuscola County Medical Society. Dr. Olin was likewise appointed as the county's delegate to the Michigan State Medical Society. [68]

In the reorganization of the Strohauer Company, Dr. Olin acquired a majority stake. After the transfer of stock, he was elected president, with W. O. Luce as vice-president and E. W. Bowles as secretary and treasurer. These three, along with T. C. and J. W. Quinn, formed the board of directors. The entire stockholder group consisted of these gentlemen and two employees. [69]

In August 1909, the genial Dr. Olin resigned from his position as Caro Trustee, with William Owen stepping in to fill the role. Dr. Olin's numerous enterprises demanded much of his time, making it difficult for him to adequately fulfill his trustee duties. [70]

At this time, the Olin family was living in the house at 219, now 123, North State Street in Caro, that soon would be the W. J. Moore House.

By 1909, the Olin's tore down the old Dr. Graves House on Lot 6, Block 9, and built the magnificent Carriage House, now the W. J. Moore Garage, on Lot 3, Block 9. This was then the most celebrated home in Caro.

---

[65] Tuscola County Advertiser. June 21, 1907.
[66] Tuscola County Advertiser. March 6, 1908.
[67] Tuscola County Advertiser. March 20, 1908.
[68] Tuscola County Advertiser. April 17, 1908.
[69] Tuscola County Advertiser. July 2, 1909.
[70] Tuscola County Advertiser. August 13, 1909.

Richard Milo Olin was a multifaceted individual who had a wonderful career as a physician in Caro.

He went on to serve as the Michigan Health Commissioner and later as the Health Services Director at Michigan State University.

He was highly loved and admired by all who met him.

His contributions to Caro and the State of Michigan were significant and impactful.

Nellie Jenks

Nellie Blanch Jenks was born on April 21, 1875, in Silver Springs, New York.

Known for her outgoing and friendly nature, she was highly regarded within social gatherings.

January 1910, Nellie Olin hosted a delightful sleigh party in Caro, entertaining eight ladies. Following the festivities, they gathered at her beautiful home at 219, now 123, North Almer Street, where they played cards and enjoyed refreshments. [71]

When she and her husband went to work at Michigan State College, now the university, Nellie Olin assumed the role of supervisor of Off-campus Housing.

During the summer months, the Olin's resided in Traverse City, Michigan.

Her husband, Richard M. Olin, served as health director at Michigan State College until his passing in 1938.

Nellie Olin passed away March 18, 1955, in Lansing, Michigan.

Sale of Olin House

November 11, 1911, Dr. Richard & Nellie Olin, residents of Caro, sold to Edward N. Bliss of Columbia, Tuscola County, the West ½ of Lot 4 & 5, the North ½ of Lot 8, and Lots 3, 6, & 7, Block 9, for the consideration of $8,000. [72]

Two years later, on October 27, 1913, Edward & Myrtie Bliss sold Lots 3, 6, & 7 and the North ½ of 8, Block, to Hattie M. Talbott who was acting as the trustee of the last will and testament of Rachel B. McNair.

The price was $7,500. [73]

April 10, 1914, Lots 3, 6 &7 and North ½ of Lot 8, Block 9, were sold to William J. Moore from the Estate of Rachel McNair.

The price was $4,550. [74]

---

[71] Tuscola County Advertiser. January 23, 1910.
[72] Tuscola County Register of Deeds. Liber 158. Pg. 95.
[73] Tuscola County Register of Deeds. Liber 163. Pg. 76.
[74] Tuscola County Register of Deeds. Liber 164. Pg. 6.

The picture above, taken around 1914, shows the Olin House in its original glory.

The garage in the back left, recently completed at the time, complements the farm-style architecture of the Olin House perfectly.

When the house was owned by the W. J. Moore family, it underwent significant remodeling between 1923 and 1927.

Before and during this period, the W. J. Moore family was likewise transforming the yard, creating a beautifully landscaped environment.

The result was a storybook, or fairytale, wonderland that remains enchanting to this day, capturing the imagination and charm of an earlier era.

Lansing, Michigan

After establishing a successful practice, becoming involved in local politics, and living ten years in Caro, Dr. Richard Olin and his family relocated to Lansing, Michigan.

In 1917, the governor of the State of Michigan appointed Dr. Olin as the Secretary of the Michigan Board of Health.

In 1919, a new law was passed by the state legislature.

It dissolved the State Board of Health and replaced it with the State Health Commissioner position. [75]

Dr. Olin likewise was appointed to this role by the governor.

He was tasked with overseeing the implementation and enforcement of health laws across the state.

During this period, the devastating "Spanish Flu" pandemic swept through Michigan as it did worldwide, causing extensive illness.

Now, in his capacity with the State of Michigan, Dr. Olin spearheaded aggressive public health initiatives aimed at controlling infectious diseases.

Despite his transition to a statewide role, he remained well-regarded for his medical expertise that began with his previous treatment of ailments such as sore throats, coughs, and sneezes in Caro.

Dr. Olin's time in Caro likewise provided valuable political experience.

His innate ability to aid and assist others fostered in the City of Caro and elsewhere served him well throughout his career.

---

[75] Michigan Department of Health. New Public Health Law. Pg. 9

The Michigan State Capitol in 1914 stood proudly in a landscape that was rapidly evolving, reflecting the growth and modernization of the state.

This period marked a significant chapter in Michigan's history, as the state government expanded its reach and influence.

Among the prominent figures working within the Capitol was Dr. Richard Milo Olin, who served as Michigan Health Commissioner.

Dr. Olin's office was a hub of activity and innovation, where he oversaw public health initiatives that aimed to improve the well-being of Michigan's residents.

His work was instrumental in addressing the health challenges of the time, and his dedication to public service left a lasting impact on the state's healthcare system.

The Capitol, with its grand architecture and bustling environment, was not just a symbol of governance but also a center for progressive change and public welfare, encapsulating the spirit of a state on the move.

Michigan State University

Olin Health Center is familiar to many who attended Michigan State University.

Following his tenure as secretary of the State Board of Health and later acting as the Michigan Health Commissioner, Dr. Olin became Michigan State University's first full-time physician.

In 1925, Dr. Olin assumed the role of Health Services Director at Michigan State University.

It was a position he held until his passing in 1938.

Throughout his tenure, he served as the physician for the Michigan State University's football team.

He accompanied the team on many out-of-town trips.

Dr. Olin's dedication and loyalty were widely recognized by fans, players, and coaches.

During his time at Michigan State University, Dr. Olin performed a multitude of duties.

Those responsibilities included examining and vaccinating hundreds of freshmen students.

His meticulous and well-directed administration ensured that comprehensive care of the student body would be performed.

In 1939, Olin Health Center was erected in Dr. Olin's honor.

It serves as a lasting tribute to his legacy.

The journey of this country doctor, who once resided at 123 North Almer Street, Caro, we remember, fondly.

His contributions we cherished with heartfelt appreciation. [76]

---

[76] Michigan State College Record. 1938. Pg. 18.

Above is the Michigan State University—Olin Memorial Hospital, a facility that continues to serve the community today as the Olin Health Center. This institution stands as a testament to the enduring legacy of Dr. Richard Milo Olin, who played a pivotal role in its establishment and development.

Dr. Olin's journey to becoming a revered figure in Michigan's medical community began in the City of Caro, where he worked as a country physician.

The transition from country physician to a prominent figure at Michigan State University symbolizes Dr. Olin's significant contributions to the field of medicine and public health.

The Olin Memorial Hospital, now the Olin Health Center, stands as a beacon of his legacy, providing essential health services to the university community and beyond. This center continues to embody Dr. Olin's vision of accessible, high-quality healthcare, ensuring that his impact on the health and well-being of Michigan's residents endures to this day.

William James Moore & Lovila Ellen Wooley

April 10, 1914, William J. & Lovila Moore bought from the Rachel B. McNair Estate Lots 3, 6, 7, and the North ½ of Lot 8, Block 9, in the City of Caro.

The consideration was 4,550. [77]

W. J. Moore's Early Life

W. J. Moore's parents were Samuel Kinsey Moore, who was a lumberman, and Elizabeth Selina Fox, who brought life and happiness to the family.

In 1875, at the age of five, W. J. Moore relocated to Michigan's Thumb region with his family.

Settling in Sandusky, he grew up initially showing an interest in following in his father's footsteps in the business of lumbering.

W. J. Moore received an early education in Saginaw before pursuing an Accountancy Diploma at International Business College in Saginaw.

He would briefly attend Oberlin College from 1889 to 1890.

He soon was drawn to the emerging industry of telephones having been inspired by his cousin, Elisha Gray, the renowned inventor.

While at Oberlin, Moore dedicated spare time to experimenting with phone devices.

He focused particularly on transmitter technology.

He obtained a patent for a transmitter in 1896 at the age of 26.

He then established two businesses in 1892 based on the invention.

The gadget proved highly successful and brought considerable revenue. [78]

---

[77] Tuscola County Register of Deeds. Liber 164, Pg. 6.
[78] Manuscript written by W. J. Moore. November 4, 1951.

Pictured above circa 1905, William James Moore, a resident of Caro, Michigan, lived a life full of promise and potential. His presence in the community was marked by a blend of entrepreneurial spirit and civic dedication, making him a prominent figure in the town's development during the early 20th century.

William James Moore's life was a testament to the power of vision, hard work, and community spirit. His contributions to Caro, Michigan, left a legacy, demonstrating what can be achieved when one lives a life of promise and purpose. Even today, the impact of his work continues to be felt, a lasting tribute to a man who helped shape the future of Caro, Michigan.

Initial Work

William James Moore, known commonly as "W. J. Moore," was affectionately called "Bill" by his family.

He made considerable contributions to the Thumb region of Michigan and the welcoming City of Caro.

W. J. Moore was born in the same town as telephone inventor Alexander Graham Bell.

W. J. Moore likewise was the cousin of telephone co-inventor Elisha Gray who founded the Western Electric Company.

Renowned for his mastery of gadgets, the ingenuity of W. J. Moore rivaled that of Alexander Bell.

In 1896, W. J. Moore founded the Moore Telephone System and the Moore Telephone Manufacturing Company.

W. J. Moore not only supplied telephones but also offered phone services to numerous customers throughout the western Thumb region—initially, hotels and stores were the primary users of the services.

As the demand for home phone services surged, W. J. Moore's two businesses grew exponentially.

By 1894, many Bell Telephone System patents expired but the company retained patents on many aspects of early telephone technology.

Moore Telephone System, however, successfully provided services to the Upper Thumb of Michigan as W. J. Moore held his own patents.

Initially, with little competition, W. J. Moore provided services in Sandusky and Marlette, Michigan.

In 1896, Moore Telephone Manufacturing Company relocated to Caro.

It continued to manufacture phones and associated equipment.

At the same time, Moore Telephone System offered exchange or network services and soon moved its operations to Caro.

W. J. Moore Companies

Early in the telephone industry, W. J. Moore owned exchanges in Sandusky and Marlette, Michigan.

W. J. Moore would later sell these two branches to the Bell Telephone Company.

W. J. Moore had presented an offer to the Caro Council that proposed that his company build an exchange initially with forty subscribers in the Caro area at a cost of $1,200 and a total capital of $2,000.

Moore Phones were priced at $15 and estimated yearly service costs were $200 per subscriber—each share in the company entitled a person to have a connection with a line to the **Moore Telephone System**.

The Moore Telephone System office would be in Caro—the offer was deemed a great opportunity for the community of Caro.

Discussions arose regarding the **Moore Telephone Manufacturing Company**— W. J. Moore struck a deal with the citizens of Caro.

For $5,000, the manufacturing operation likewise would be relocated to Caro—it was agreed upon and the result was that every party including the manufacturing company flourished—the sales of Moore Phones expanded to almost every state in the United States.

In 1915, W. J. Moore sold Moore Telephone Manufacturing Company at its peak and when his patents neared expiration.

In 1946, Moore Telephone System incorporated—W. J. Moore's youngest son, Andrew, was appointed president and manager—it was a family-owned business. W. J. Moore retained interest in the corporation and was given the title of consulting engineer.

Over time, Moore Telephone System expanded and established over twenty exchanges across Michigan.

Subscriptions grew from 10 in 1892 to 2,500 in 1947 when capital was $50,000 and employees numbered 30 people. Each month, Moore Telephone Systems brought in $5,000 in revenue. [79]

---

[79] Tuscola County Advertiser. June 24, 1955.

Moore Interests

In addition to his dedication to the telephone industry, W. J. Moore likewise participated in various other business enterprises.

W. J. Moore was the director and largest stockholder of the Caro State Savings Bank.

He likewise held a leadership position in both the Moore Subdivision and the W. J. Moore real estate businesses. [80]

The impact of the endeavors of W. J. Moore and his family members represents much of what the City of Caro epitomizes from the past and likewise today.

We are a charitable and giving community—we all need to exchange a deep expression of gratitude to each other.

W. J. Moore as well was active in several non-profit organizations: the Telephone Pioneers of America and the Independent Telephone Association of America.

He took part in the activities of the Caro Chamber of Commerce and Caro Exchange Club.

Outside professional pursuits both for profit and non-profit, W. J. Moore and his family had a variety of hobbies: photography, landscape gardening, motorcars, and of course swimming.

Later in life, W. J. Moore was given the accolated "Gadget Man." This was due to his passion for tinkering and inventing.

As he grew old, W. J. Moore gradually shifted focus away from business operations and again towards inventive endeavors.

The restructuring of Moore Telephone System allowed W. J. Moore to again devote time to developing new gadgets that would benefit himself and others.

In 1947, after nearly 60 years in the communication, the phone business, W. J. Moore retired.

---

[80] Manuscript of W. J. Moore. November 4, 1951.

The Moore Telephone System office, situated at 201 Montague Street in Caro, served as a pivotal communication hub, facilitating the connection and exchange of personal, business, and urgent calls.

This office was more than just a building; it was the nerve center of Caro's communication network, reflecting the rapid technological advancements of the early 20th century.

In an era when the telephone was transforming how people connected, the Moore Telephone System office enabled residents to stay in touch with loved ones, conduct business efficiently, and respond quickly to emergencies.

Operators worked diligently at switchboards, connecting calls with precision, ensuring that the community remained linked to both local and distant contacts.

For local businesses, the office was indispensable, providing a reliable means to communicate with suppliers, customers, and partners.

This facilitated economic growth and fostered commercial relationships.

The ability to swiftly handle urgent calls underscored the office's role in maintaining public safety and coordinating responses during critical moments.

The Moore Telephone System office symbolized progress and modernity, showcasing Caro's integration into the broader technological landscape.

It was a hub of activity, where the convergence of personal, commercial, and emergency communications highlighted its essential place in the fabric of the community.

Amid the spools of telephone wire, the W. J. Moore family pauses to strengthen their familial bonds and contemplate the future that lies ahead.

The setting, surrounded by the intricate web of communication lines that define their business, offers a moment of respite from the bustling activity of their daily endeavors.

Here, amidst the tangible symbols of their enterprise, they come together to share moments of reflection, conversation, and unity.

In the photograph above, on the left side, early telephone operators are seen diligently working, ensuring that calls are connected smoothly and communication flows seamlessly.

Meanwhile, on the right side of the image, W. J. Moore is depicted sitting at his desk, engrossed in deep contemplation and review.

He carefully considers not only what is best for himself but also for his employees and the broader community as he strategizes for the future.

The Operator Room, also known as the Exchange or Network Room, within the Moore Telephone System, served as the bustling hub where all connections were made. This room was the heart of activity, where operators worked tirelessly to facilitate communication through the telephone network.

In this essential space, operators manned switchboards, managing incoming and outgoing calls with precision and efficiency. They were responsible for connecting callers within Caro and beyond, using manual switchboards to establish direct lines between different telephone subscribers. Each operator was trained to handle multiple calls simultaneously, ensuring that connections were established promptly and accurately.

Overall, the Operator Room of the Moore Telephone System was integral to the functioning of Caro's telecommunications infrastructure. It embodied the dedication and expertise of the operators who played a pivotal role in connecting people, businesses, and emergency services throughout the community and beyond.

De Dion-Bouton

The W. J. Moore family's fascination with automobiles was captivating.

In 1899, they became the owner of De Dion-Bouton that they imported from France to arrive in Caro—De Dion Bouton was the first automobile, or horseless carriage, in Michigan's Thumb.

On the opposite page to this narrative, is the depiction of De Dion-Bouton—the Moore family's first car.

The depiction comes from early summer of 1899.

It shows De Dion Bouton in front of the Moore Telephone System office in Caro—the office was established only a few years earlier.

De Dion-Bouton arrived in Caro from France where it was enclosed in a large box lined with oiled paper—De Dion Bouton journeyed here by way of a steamer or steam ship.

On arrival, De Dion-Bouton when being unpacked was met by the local crowd—it may have been half the population of Caro that gathered to celebrate the occasion of the arrival of De Dion-Bouton.

The Moore family later created a replica of De Dion-Bouton on the facade of the family garage in remembrance where they could see it with a quick glance.

De Dion Bouton eventually went to a museum.

Subsequently, the cars owned by the Moore family included a 1906 Olds Palace Touring car followed by Buicks and Fords—they all served purposes that were both business and leisure.

In 1914, W. J. Moore ordered an automobile that was custom-made and equipped with W. J. Moore's acclaimed world's first auto-telephone—it was a Cadillac.

The first of the families' Cadillacs was a custom made 51 V8—1915—subsequently, they acquired several more Cadillacs—the Moore family had great pride in all their automobiles. [81]

---

[81] Manuscript of the Moore Family.

In the photograph, W. J. Moore is seated in De Dion-Bouton alongside Warren Olin, who served as the Superintendent of Moore Telephone System.

They are positioned in front of the Moore Telephone System office, likely contemplating a race in the automobile, perhaps at the Tuscola County Fairground to add a change of pace.

Olin later became the proprietor of Olin & Son Drug Store.

Notably, W. J. Moore participated in races with the modified De Dion Bouton at the fairground. The most significant race ended in a tie, as recounted by many.

Cadillac Model 51 V8 - 1915

The Moore Cadillac boasted—it had an array of luxurious features: a heater, air-conditioning, reversing lights, pneumatic shock absorbers, refrigerator, swivel seats, double bed, and a telephone—it was a true embodiment of opulence. The touring sedan was equipped with every conceivable amenity. W. J. Moore ingeniously devised a method of using the car's telephone by parking it next to a telephone pole and connecting it to the telephone line with a long tube.

The sedan's body was designed by W. J. Moore and constructed by C. P. Kimball & Company of Chicago. The motor was the first of its kind to feature 8-cylinders and was built by the Cadillac Motor Company. Accommodating a driver and seven passengers, the car's stationary rear seating area boasted three comfortable seats. The remaining four seats were arranged in two rows forward of the back seats. It resembled Pullman-style seats that could be adjusted forward and backward on slides that were attached to the floor. Additionally, the center seats could rotate in any direction.

The sedan's innovative design allowed for versatile seating arrangements, including transforming the back three and center two seats into a two-person bed. Alternatively, it could be a bed for one person. Utilizing a circulation tube and thirteen vents, warm air from the radiator quickly entered the interior during cold weather.

A stove near the radiator provided heating when the engine was not running. Electric fans ensured that the air would circulate.

Behind the rear seat, a refrigerator stored food. During the summer months, regulated fans drew air from the refrigerator to cool the interior of the car.

All ten windows featured tight-setting roller shades that enhanced privacy and comfort. Dubbed a "cozy living room on wheels," the Moore sedan was admired by all who laid eyes on it. It provided an unparalleled riding experience. Additionally, it was equipped with telescopic tubes, binoculars, and a camera.

The Moore family, along with the community of Caro and Tuscola County, took great pride in this remarkable vehicle.

The Cadillac currently resides in the Louwman Automobile Museum in The Hague, Netherlands.

The 1915 Cadillac Model 51 V8 pictured above is a testament to the ingenuity and design prowess of W. J. Moore.

This automobile was a marvel of its time, featuring an array of advanced gadgets that showcased the innovation and engineering expertise of the era.

It represented a significant achievement in automotive design, setting new standards for performance and technology in the early 20th century.

Lovila Ellen Wooley

Lovila Moore, originally from Springfield, Ontario, moved to Marlette, Michigan, with her parents when she was ten years old.

November 4, 1896, she married William James Moore and relocated to Caro.

Known for her gracious manner and generous hospitality, she often hosted gatherings with open arms.

In 1934, she hosted a gathering for 160 ladies from Sanilac, Huron, and Tuscola counties to organize a political club in support of her chosen gubernatorial candidate. Politically active and compassionate, Lovila Moore made significant contributions and provided solace to many.

Following her passing on May 28, 1937, a large group of friends gathered to attend her funeral at the beautiful Moore House, where she had demonstrated her organizational skills and congenial nature.

The funeral was adorned with a wealth of flowers, a testament to the esteem in which she was held.

On June 1, 1939, W. J. Moore married Mabel Clark in Evart, Michigan.

Children:

1. Claude. He was the oldest and died at Ann Arbor in 1918 as a member of the Student Army Training Corps in World War I—1899-1918.
2. Earl. He lived in Detroit, Michigan—1902-1984.
3. Vera. She married Fred Graham, and they operated a theater in Chesaning, Michigan—1903-1975.
4. Maurice. —1910-1946.
5. Andrew. As a graduate of Civil Engineering at Michigan State College, he became the president of Moore Telephone System. Later, he and wife Dolores Nugent owned the W. J. Moore House that they cherished—1911-1971.

At this time, the Moore family was the most beloved and respected family in Caro.

It was the best of times.

W. J. and Lovila

William J. Moore and Lovila E. Wooley's marriage in 1896 marked a significant milestone in their lives, symbolizing hope and possibility for the future. In an era defined by optimism and burgeoning opportunities, their union reflected the aspirations of a young couple embarking on life's journey together. The late 19th century was a period of rapid industrialization and social change, where innovation and progress seemed limitless. Against this backdrop, William and Lovila Moore's marriage epitomized the dreams and ambitions of many young people at the time, seeking to build a prosperous and fulfilling life. Their commitment to each other not only represented personal happiness but also embodied the spirit of optimism and potential that characterized the turn of the century.

Remodeling the W. J. Moore House

April 10, 1914, W. J. & Lovila Moore acquired the property at 219, or now 123, North Almer Street from the McNair Estate.

Even before 1914, it was one of the finest residences in Caro, though its appearance differed from how it looks today.

Prior to the Moore family's alterations, the property boasted a lush yard with abundant shade and a charming stable, along with a garage for carriages and multiple automobiles.

Formerly the residence of the Dr. Olin family, it provided exceptional comfort and sophistication at that time.

By 1914, the home featured hardwood walls and floors, hot water heating, ample plumbing, and a delightful outdoor setting.

In 1916, the Moore family undertook various improvements, including tree trimming, building painting, and installing a heating system in the garage.

They also added a tennis court for recreational purposes and planted mature trees and numerous shrubs.

The highlight was the construction of a private swimming pool in 1916, which garnered much attention in the community of Caro.

Beginning in 1923 and until 1927, the Moore family applied a stunning stone exterior to the property.

Claude A. Putnam, a local stonemason, contributed significantly to this transformation. As payment for his work, he received a new communication device—the telephone—supplied by the Moore family.

Throughout the remodeling process, workers were paid 67 cents per hour, with masons and painters earning higher wages.

Notable individuals involved in the project included Harry Parsell, who handled much of the decorating and painting, and Seymour Kelly, the head carpenter, assisted by Otis Hamilton, Frank Berry, and others.

The project began in 1923 and spanned four years, during which time the Moore family resided in the club above the garage.

The equipment used to transplant trees onto the W. J. Moore property was capable of handling substantial loads.

Working in the woods, one might encounter both frogs and toads amid the task of hauling trees, which was hard and dirty work.

The construction of the W. J. Moore House was inspired and reflected the ultimate joy that comes from accomplishing a difficult task with dedication and perseverance.

Such endeavors as transplanting trees often require energy and perspiration, but they are always worth the effort, and from challenges like these, we should never shy away.

The trees, transported by dray horses, make their way along the roadway,

Traveling the winter road to reach the W. J. Moore House on a cloudy and icy day.

The horses snort and tromp through fields where partridge or prairie grouse may lie.

Oh, to revisit that time,

It would surely lift my spirits high.

The rhythmic sounds of hooves and the skates of the sled create a lovely, nostalgic rhyme.

Let's raise a toast to the W. J. Moore House.

Let's celebrate every tree that has found its place and taken root.

The trees planted at the W. J. Moore House are a delightful sight indeed.

Events like these remind us of the goodness in life.

Being outdoors, we feel the fresh air—nature's sweet kiss.

Everyone marvels at the beauty of trees.

It's heartbreaking when a tree topples, so let's embrace and cherish them.

Let's give them the love and care they deserve.

Working on the W. J. Moore House required exceptional skill and competence—everyone rose to the challenge.

In those days, workers didn't wear safety glasses or dust masks.

They were at the peak of their abilities, often lifting heavy stones and scaling ladders.

The work was perilous at times.

One might say, "There were moments of hazard."

Yet, they persevered.

Soon, a fairytale or storybook land emerged before their eyes.

Remodeling or recreating the back of the W. J. Moore House as seen from the West Lincoln and North Almer Street intersection was a work of transformation.

In the end, it was a joy.

Today, the W. J. Moore House is a fairyland for any girl or boy.

Much time was spent getting things done right, and now the W. J. Moore House attracts many admirers, day and night.

Here, life is at its best.

Life is good at the W. J. Moore House and in the surrounding fairytale forest.

Life is at its finest.

Moore House Activities

Upon completion, the Moore House featured a spacious garage capable of housing up to fifteen automobiles. Additionally, it included dressing rooms for swimmers utilizing the pool. The property boasted three driveways and a replica model of the first car—De Dion Bouton—ever driven in Tuscola County mounted on the garage. Furthermore, there was a sizable club room above the garage suitable for playing basketball, which served as a venue for the sport for students until Caro constructed its new High School.

The Moore House stood out as a marvel of architectural ingenuity in Caro, captivating both locals and visitors alike with its enchanting appearance.

Universally admired as a beautiful fairytale creation, it remains a source of admiration for present generations, evoking fond memories from our parents and grandparents.

Concealed behind lush green hedges, the house witnessed numerous grand gatherings and lavish parties in days gone by. On Sunday afternoons, family, relatives, and friends would convene, filling the rooms and benches around the pool with lively conversations and camaraderie.

W. J. Moore's inventive spirit was evident throughout the house. Controlled by a master electrical control panel in the side hall were numerous door-openers and burglar alarms adorning its interiors. Among his remarkable creations was a mechanical trapeze that transported swimmers from the second-floor bedrooms directly into the swimming pool.

As a telephone entrepreneur, W. J. Moore outfitted the house with twenty-two telephones and an array of gadgetry, ensuring communication access in every room. The attic, spacious and well-appointed, formed a significant part of the layout of the house.

The grounds surrounding the house were a botanical marvel, with beautiful flowers blooming in abundance. From the grass tennis court to the water fountain, the yard and gardens exuded an air of tranquility and charm, reminiscent of scenes from Disney movies and fairytale books.

"Back in 1927, passersby viewed the W. J. Moore residence with curiosity and awe." [82]

---

[82] Tuscola Advertiser. March 18, 1965.

The view of the W. J. Moore House from across North Almer Street is truly enchanting,

Eliciting fanciful melodies reminiscent of nostalgic tunes heard at county fairs on warm summer days.

It fills one with a playful whimsy, tempting you to toss coins into the air,

Yet with a thought for practicality, reserving some for popcorn, a hotdog, or a jar of honey—embracing such fanciful moments with care.

You rein in these whimsical thoughts, holding them in check,

While the wind around the W. J. Moore House whispers its rhythmic serenade,

Occasionally interrupted by the solemn clanging of nearby church bells, hinting at a discordant note.

These moments define enchantment, capturing the essence of a truly magical experience.

W. J. Moore House Remembered

The W. J. Moore House hosted extravagant lawn and pool gatherings that epitomized the opulence of its era.

As evening fell, guests congregated around one or more of the five fireplaces within the house, enjoying cozy conversations in a warm ambiance. Operated entirely by electricity, the house boasted modern amenities, including an electric dishwasher, ventilator, and ice freezer in the kitchen. Comprising five bedrooms, three bathrooms, a living room, radio room, den, kitchen, laundry area, and maid's quarters, the house provided ample living space. Air conditioning was available in the living, dining, and radio rooms, as well as the front hallway.

Outdoor electric lights illuminated the tennis court, fountain, rock garden, swimming pool, and garage at night, while a sophisticated burglar system alerted law enforcement immediately upon activation.

The garage, crafted with inlaid stone and wood, could accommodate up to fifteen automobiles. Upstairs, the clubhouse hosted dancing, amateur plays, and high school basketball games, serving as a versatile entertainment venue.

The property, meticulously designed, exuded beauty and grace, with rustic benches, lush flowers, and stone pillars surrounding the pool.

An impressive fifteen-foot glass aquarium housed multicolored Japanese fish, while a large waterfall adorned the rock garden along Almer Street.

A path led to the Japanese bridge, which provided access to the dressing rooms at the pool's west end. A stone lighthouse, featuring a small metal gnome carrying a lantern and lance, added whimsical charm to the landscape. The lighthouse guard atop the structure captivated onlookers when illuminated, drawing more than just passing glances.

Constructed from stones native to the Thumb area, the forty-foot chimney at the garage was a testament to local craftsmanship. The estate's evergreen hedge featured posts made of large stones, while a specially designed machine, created by Mr. Moore, facilitated the transplantation of elm trees throughout the yard. Martin birdhouses were strategically placed around the property, further enhancing its natural charm. [83]

---

[83] Tuscola Advertiser. March 18, 1965.

This photograph exudes classic elegance.

It's almost grandiloquent or bombastic in its portrayal.

How could a house appear so impeccably grand?

The trees and walkway seem to whisper tales of the past.

Everything exudes loftiness and grace, akin to a beautifully sung melody.

This view of the W. J. Moore House evokes tears, for those early days now gone, a truth undeniable.

It captures the W. J. Moore House at its zenith.

It stirs emotions that linger, reminding us of its enduring beauty.

A light at night pierces through time's veil,

Recalling when the W. J. Moore House stood tall and hale.

In an era of mechanical and electrical sway,

Now eclipsed by the digital age's display.

Dark nights echo those bygone days of old,

When children swam for just a coin's hold.

Light and darkness, virtues and vices intertwine,

Contrasts in life's tapestry often align.

Zippy zip, from the balcony take flight . . . Overlooking the pool in the moonlight.

The W. J. Moore House airplane and zipline, old-school delight . . . An experience with a dash of fright.

It's a dream to zoom . . . . To step from the balcony and leave your room,

Dropping into the water . . . nothing is better . . . A childhood memory, for an adventurous go-getter.

The living room is adorned with a rustic stone fireplace,

Creating a cozy and inviting space.

It's ideal for relaxation and enjoyment,

Where you can unwind without fear,

Savor the moment,

And sit close to those you hold dear.

Experience the tranquility,

Enjoy the serenity.

The rounded eaves of the W. J. Moore House do not shelter fairies,

Fairies dwell in the open air, not within.

They belong to days long past,

Whispering tales of beauty from ancient times.

Legends speak of their presence among the hedges,

A sight that captivates all who behold them.

The W. J. Moore House stands as a sanctuary of simplicity,

Where memories bloom with the hue of nostalgia.

Later Owners

Andrew J. & Dolores Moore

On March 7, 1911, Andrew Moore was welcomed into the family of William J. & Lovila Moore.

Alongside his wife Dolores, Andrew was an active member of Caro's St. Paul's Lutheran Church.

When they resided at 123 North Almer Street, they remained connected to the cherished memories of the W. J. Moore House.

From their elevated balcony, they relished the view and the vibrant tales that surrounded this esteemed residence.

Andrew Moore eventually assumed the role of manager and owner of Moore Telephone System upon his father's retirement, continuing the family's legacy of service to Caro and the Michigan Thumb region.

The marriage of Andrew Moore & Dolores Nugent took place on June 5, 1935, in Bad Axe, Michigan. Dolores passed away in June 1957.

Andrew found companionship again when he married Hildegarde Felske Boesenecker on July 26, 1958, a respected teacher in Caro.

Together, they contributed to the Caro community, with Hildegarde's annual tours of the W. J. Moore House becoming a cherished tradition for students and a labor of love for her.

Andrew Moore's involvement extended beyond Caro, as he was an esteemed member of the Michigan State University Association.

Andrew Moore's passing on June 29, 1971, marked the end of an era, but his contributions to Caro and beyond endured in the hearts and minds of many.

Children:

1. Gerald James. He was born in 1936 in Caro, Michigan. He died in 2001 in Mesa Arizona.
2. Robert Claude. Robert was born in 1941 in Caro, Michigan. He died in 2009 in Mesa, Arizona.

Andrew and Dolores Moore, pictured with their son Gerald in Andrew's arms, epitomized the essence of familial charm and unity. Gerald, nestled in his father's embrace, symbolized the joy and hope that the Moore family cherished.

This photograph captures a moment of warmth and love, reflecting the deep bond between parents and child.

Andrew and Dolores Moore, known for their dedication to family and community, instilled values of love, compassion, and resilience in their son Gerald, ensuring that the legacy of the Moore family continued with grace and strength.

Charles & Dorcas Vaughan

The Vaughan family purchased the W. J. Moore house in 1966. [84]

According to the Caro Phone Books from 1966 and 1969, the property, now known as 123 North Almer Street, had previously been listed as 219 N. Almer Street.

The Vaughans dedicated significant time and resources to preserving and maintaining the W. J. Moore House, keeping it in pristine condition.

Their commitment to the house was evident in their willingness to undertake necessary repairs and upkeep.

Following in the footsteps of the Moore family, the Vaughans welcomed neighborhood children to swim in the pool, enhancing the house's reputation as a local treasure.

The W. J. Moore House was a celebrated home for the Vaughans. [85]

Sunday school children delighted in their visits to what they fondly called the Vaughan "Disney House," feeling as though they had stepped into a playful wonderland.

The Vaughans also employed a local disabled person, Floyd Evans, to care for the landscape and lawn, reflecting their strong community spirit and generosity.

Dorcas Dorman, a graduate of Central Michigan University, taught in local rural schools for five years.

Chuck Vaughan attended country school and began working for the W. N. Clark Company at 17. He enlisted in the Navy during World War II and married Dorcas on July 6, 1947. At 21, Chuck partnered with his uncle, Ted Vaughan, in the sand and gravel business.

Chuck & Dorcas Vaughan diversified their business interests, engaging in sand and gravel ventures in both Michigan and Florida, as well as operating campgrounds, motels, subdivisions, game ranches, and a restaurant.

---

[84] Tuscola Advertiser. July 17, 2017.
[85] Tuscola County Register of Deeds. Liber 1224, Pg. 1105.

Linda & Kim Vaughan

On April 1, 2008, Dorcas and Charles Vaughan transferred ownership of the former W. J. Moore House to their son, Kim, via a Quit Claim Deed.

In earlier times, it was not uncommon for family members to sell property for $1 and other valuable considerations.

Kim Vaughan, known for his raspy, deep, and powerful voice, loves to discuss his beliefs, faith, and creed.

The Vaughans developed recreational and residential parks in Florida and Michigan, with Kim emerging as a natural leader.

He is actively involved in politics and serves as the Chairperson of the Tuscola County Board of Commissioners.

Kim Vaughan married Linda Ziemba.

Melissa & Alvin Zavitz

In October of 2020, Melissa & Alvin Zavitz bought 123 North Almer Street, the W. J. Moore House, from Linda & Kim Vaughan. [86]

The amount of $215,000 was the consideration.

The American Auto Sales & Service south of Millington was owned by the Zavitz family.

To show gratitude, Alvin Zavtiz became a Caro City Council member.

Melisa Zavitz was a Caro Community Schools teacher.

---

[86] Ibid. Liber 1378, Pg. 133.

Steve & Becky Shields

The current owners of the W. J. Moore House are Steve & Becky Shields.

Steve Shields is the great-great-grandson of W. J. & Lovila Moore.

August 23, 2021, he and his wife, Becky, fulfilled a long-held dream by purchasing the W. J. Moore house, a significant part of his heritage.

Steve's mother, Tamara Moore Elenbaum, is the daughter of Gerald J. Moore, who was the son of Andrew J. Moore, the youngest child of W. J. and Lovila Moore.

Since acquiring the house, the couple has brought new life to the property.

In June 2022, the W. J. Moore House, along with its grounds and carriage house, or garage, was opened for "Community Tours."

That same weekend, the History Channel TV show "American Pickers" filmed an episode on-site.

In June 2023, the Community Tour was expanded to two days, with additional parts of the house made accessible to visitors.

Many historical items associated with the W. J. Moore House were displayed, and stories about the family were shared.

In March 2024, the W. J. Moore House was listed on the National Register of Historic Places.

The W. J. Moore House offers a wonderful glimpse into early life in Caro and allows visitors to experience the enchanting dreams that reside in our minds and hearts through tours and events held there.

Under the care of Steve and Becky Shields, the W. J. Moore House is in good hands.

They can see this through.

They will ensure that for generations to come, the W. J. Moore House stands strong.

Regarding the property, they always have a wonderful view.

Steve and Becky Shields enjoy playing with their dogs.

Steve finds fulfillment in graphic arts.

They diligently maintain the preservation of the W. J. Moore House, overcoming any obstacles.

Their dedication is unparalleled.

Having descendants of the Moore family involved ensures the spirit of the W. J. Moore House remains vibrant and alive!

Under their continued leadership, it is certain that the business of local history will thrive.

Post Log

Local residents and guests alike love to recall, read, and recite the tales and realities from the W. J. Moore House. When W. J. Moore and his family entertained, with other notable figures, visiting, it was a time of glory and excitement.

The house at 123 North Almer Street is a cherished destination for many, drawing visitors both past and present. The W. J. Moore House, with its vintage "Hollywood Style" pool, its intricate stonework, and its enduring charm, entices everyone. We dream of taking the old airplane ride from the balcony, gliding over the pool, and plunging into the water with laughter and a bit of fright.

People once flocked to listen to W. J. Moore speak, captivated by his words, both adults and children alike. On Saturday afternoons, local children could swim in the pool for just 5 cents, bringing delight, in their screaming and dancing, to the community.

The W. J. Moore House offers a fantastic glimpse into Caro's past, making it the perfect place to step back in time. It embodies the spirit of the Caro community, refreshing the mind and soul, and highlighting the best goals in life. Owned by many influential people, the W. J. Moore House property is a symbol of life in Caro and stands unparalleled. Its timbers may date back to the foundation of Caro, originally known as Centreville.

Today, the W. J. Moore House stands tall as a fairytale or Disney-style home, recalling the romantic and gilded life on which the town was built. It resonates with the stories of Caro, the West Gateway to the Thumb of Michigan. The W. J. Moore family exemplifies the importance of good communication, and the house itself seems to echo with unique sounds and stories.

The W. J. Moore House remains a place of rich information exchange, uplifting the Caro community. The best guardian of this resonant place can only be a descendant of the W. J. Moore family, dedicated to restoring and preserving its valuable history and passing on its legacy.

The W. J. Moore House narrates a tale of deep significance. It acts as a crucial hub for idea exchange, aiding in the confrontation of forthcoming challenges. Engaging with its story, observing its imagery, assimilating its information and language, and valuing its melodies enriches us all, bolstering our well-being for the present and forevermore.

Made in the USA
Columbia, SC
27 June 2024

dd17c7d8-c95a-419e-8ab5-549247e5a1a8R01